The Old Gympie Bakeries and their Families

John Stark

Reading Stones Publishing

Copyright © 2022 by R. John Stark

All rights reserved. No part may be reproduced or transmitted by any form or my any means, electronic or mechanical including photocopying, recording, or by any information storage and retrieval system, without written permission of both the copyright owner and publisher. Inquiries should be addressed to the publishers.

All photographs are the copyright of the author.

National Library of Australia Card Number and

ISBN: Soft Cover 978-0-9586138-2-8

Typeset by: Lynette Day, Gin Gin. Qld

Front Cover: Staff at front of Harry's Bakery Pty Ltd. 1946
From Left to Right:-

Tom Bradley	Horse & Cart Carter
Steve Heilbronn:	Town & Country Delivery Driver (Austin)
Ted Harry:	Owner, Baker Pastrycook.
Doug Roy:	Apprentice Baker Pastrycook.
Cliff Harry:	Owner, Baker Pastrycook.
Sid:	The Dog

In Ovals above:-

Beryl Jensen:	Office Girl.
Stan Blakeway:	Doughmaker, Baker.
Colin McBride:	Apprentice Baker
John Stark:	Apprentice Baker Pastrycook.

Bottom Photo:	Ronald (John) Stark – aged 16, 1946
Published by:	Reading Stones Publishing
	Helen and Wendy Brown
	212 Glenburnie Rd
	Rob Roy NSW 2360
	hbrown19561@gmail.com

Contents

Dedication	Page v
Disclaimer	Page vii
Foreword	Page ix
My Founding Story	Page xi

Chapter 1. — Page 1
William Thomas Weller, Widgee Crossing.

Chapter 2. — Page 8
William Thomas Weller, 179 - 183 Nashville, now Monkland.

Chapter 3. — Page 14
Russell's Bakery, 42 - 42a Iron Street, Gympie.

Chapter 4 — Page 18
Henry Long, 72 - 74 Duke Street, Gympie.

Chapter 5. — Page 23
William Weller & Son, Brisbane & Gorgie Rds, Monkland, Gympie

Chapter 6. — Page 26
James Condie, 32 - 38 Reef St, Gympie.

Chapter 7. — Page 29
W & J Condie, 32 - 38 Reef St, Gympie.

Chapter 8. — Page 38
Isaac Branch, 5, 5a, 7 Appollonian Vale, Gympie.

Chapter 9. — Page 50
Neil Bradford, 83 Red Hill Rd, Gympie.

Chapter 10. — Page 53
Reg Sherran & Sons, 5, 5a, 7 Appollonian Vale, Gympie.

Chapter 11. — Page 60
Thomas Condie, 137 Mary Street Gympie.

Chapter 12. — Page 65
Fred Weller, 261 - 263 Brisbane Rd, Monkland Gympie

Chapter 13. Page 68
Bill Blakeway, 72 – 74 Duke St, Gympie.

Chapter 14. Page 76
Thomas Condie, 11 Stewart Terrace, Gympie.

Chapter 15. Page 81
Reg Harry, 72 - 74 Duke St, Gympie.

Chapter 16. Page 89
Harry Bros, 72 - 74 Duke St, Gympie.

Chapter 17. Page 112
James Fardoolie, 5, 5a, 7 Appollonian Vale, Gympie

Chapter 18. Page 117
John Stark, Baker - Pastry Cook, Busby St, Amamoor.

Chapter 19. Page 150
Harry Bros. incorporating W & J Condie 32-38 Reef St, Gympie.

Chapter 20. Page 157
Allan, Lesley & Henry Condie, 45 Pine St, Gympie.

Chapter 21. Page 159
Bill Dunmore, 32 - 38 Reef St, Gympie.

Chapter 22. Page 161
Mrs. Kath Harry, Brown Jug Café, 79 Mary St, Gympie.

Chapter 23. Page 165
Butcher Shops around Gympie.

Chapter 24. Page 172
Cake Icing

Chapter 25. Page 184
Bakeries that have come and gone in Gympie & District

Chapter 26. Page 186
Special Memories.

Dedication

Old Bakeries & Families of Gympie

I would like to thank my daughter Lynette for her love and dedication in the compiling of this book. For her expertise in typesetting, correction of my errors and her eye for detail of colour and design. Without her help this book would never have been able to be completed in the time frame that had been set.

I would also like to thank the private persons who so willingly allowed me to interview them for their memories of the bakeries in this book.

Disclaimer

Eldor Adalbert Stark. Photo 1936

My interest in bread was more than a little fad. My father, Eldor (Ted) Stark, became the first Queensland bread vendor in 1929.

I have tried to locate the friends and families of mates that I was connected with or worked beside in the manufacture of bread.

Their stories will give a true and accountable record of bakeries in the Gympie and surrounding towns throughout the years of 1867 to 1972.

I have purchased the three complete sets of records kept by the sextons of the Gympie and District Deaths recorded for the areas of Gympie's three cemeteries, Mary Valley, Cooloola, and Kilkivan also other small interments recorded by Mrs. June Zillman of the Gympie Ancestral Research Society Inc. 1995. This society have now updated their records to 2004.

In all cases I have tried to give a true and correct record, from living and recording my life, by stories and photos. In some cases, I may have overlapped with stories from my previous books.

In some cases, I have not been able to give the person's true Christian or nicknames, as I have only the initials to go by. I have interviewed many friends to try and discover them but was unsuccessful.

Foreword

The Old Bakeries of Gympie as known by me 1867 – 1972.

The following pages outline how the people of Nashville were supplied with the lifesaving food called bread. Gold brought men from all professions and parts of the world. Would you believe that once the ships tied up in the river at Maryborough, some 80 miles (128klm) north of Gympie, they lost most of their crew to *"gold fever".*

Towns were left nearly empty. Men of all classes, colour, creed, and religion came from afar to try their luck and find this gold that was everywhere. Easily accessible, you could pick it up in the creeks and surrounding areas by hand. It was so plentiful; this dream drove them forward.

Nearly all these men carried a quantity of flour and salt, to make "duff" (damper to the modern cook). This bread allowed them to survive until they found gold and they could then buy flour and salt to make more. Everything was cooked in their cast iron camp ovens and right up to today you can go to any camping ground and see these cooking pots on nearly every open fireplace. We still have a few in my family, and the family delights in producing many scrumptious meals.

In the first 12 months, the rough town was only known as Gympie Creek, but referred to by the aborigines as Gympie Gympie (after the local stinging tree). The miners mainly called it Nashville (after James Nash who was the founder of this goldfield). It was only called this name for a few months, until officialdom under the hand of the local Acting Gold Commissioner, William Davidson, from the lands department in Maryborough ruled in favour of calling it Gympie — later retaining the area between One Mile and Monckland to have the said name of Nashville. The c in Monkland was strangely dropped by a clerk in the first court house as he referred to Monkland spelt the Irish way, which it was at first called and spelt in honour of the Scottish miners on the Gympie field. Too many official papers had been drawn up without the c in place that the officials in Gympie allowed it to stay that way, and it has stayed now for over 150 years.

I had the privilege, in the early thirties, to watch men with their rockers digging for gold in Commissioners Gully adjoining my parent's property. I watched a well-dressed gentleman in a three-piece suit working his rocker. I don't think he had any work clothes. Working over about a week, his rocker sat in the water each day and night. He had a clear glass medicine bottle with a cork in the top. Each wash he would delve into his left-hand suit pocket, pull out the bottle, and remove the cork, and place all the gold fragments into the bottle. His bottle then was half full of gold, he may have had more, I never asked him. It was impolite to ask questions like that in those days. One day he just packed up and disappeared. I can see his face clearly as if it was only yesterday. Over the intervening years I often wondered who he was, where did he come from and where did he go to from there?

The word was out, nearly 30,000 people were now on the Gympie Gold Fields over the period of years 1868 to 1900.

Many bakeries were built: I have listed them in this book, in chapter form, as I knew them to exist. Some dates of the bakeries will overlap (in years that they started), but you will be able to follow my story.

So many questions I wanted to ask over the years, I have to thank my heavenly Father, who has given me a very clear and vivid memory of my past life, thus giving my readers such a distinct version of what I have written in my past five books on Gympie's history.

The stories of Gympie's original bakeries have been on my mind for many years. My own life experiences consisted of many career changes.

My Founding Story

My Dad, Eldor Adalbert Stark, known to his friends as Ted. With his 2 mates, Harry Young and Jack Stokes, they joined the A.I.F. together in 1915 in Ipswich, Queensland and spent three and a half years in battlefields across the world, fighting in the First World War. This information is so important, as it relates to

1L-R: Harry Young, Eldor (Ted) Stark, Jack Stokes. Photo 1916/17 in France.

the friendship of these three young men. They survived the war, but they were gassed and their minds were wounded for life, but they never complained. When I joined the army in the late 1940s, my father told me a little of what to expect in the armed forces.

Before Dad left for the war, he rode up the street on his black stallion and approached a startled young lady in Kalbar and stated, "Wait for me to return from the war, Alma, and I will marry you", she was only thirteen at that time, but she knew Dad and his family well as they were close neighbours in the small town.

My mother, Alma Degener, had just started work on the haberdashery counter for Weis Brothers General store. Her father (my grandfather), Franz Degener, was the manager of the grocery section. Alma was doing her midterm finals by mail from London studying the piano. She was an accomplished pianist and also the organist for the local Methodist church all at the age of thirteen.

When the three of them returned from the war, my grandmother expected my dad to return to the family farming property, but Dad always wanted to be an engineer. His two mates returned to their parents' dairy farms and the army assisted them all in their quests.

Ted and Alma were married on the 21st April 1921. By then mother had a teaching class of 40 students.

Mum also had the first rubber-tyred sulky in the Kalbar Boonah district, and carried my eldest sister Gertrude (Trudie) in a basket on the passenger side floor, to attend her student's homes for their lessons.

Dad, again with his two friends, Harry and Jack, joined the Postmaster General's Department in Brisbane. Their first engagement was to set up telephone poles and lines in the Murgon, Proston, and Kingaroy districts. His two friends were employed as linesmen and worked beside dad. In the years 1924 to 1927, Dad, with his two mates and their families, were transferred from Murgon to Cooroy. In 1927 Gympie was being set up for phones so the three families were transferred there.

82 Horseshoe Bend

When Mother and Dad arrived in Gympie, they rented the above home in Horseshoe Bend. Harry and Jack rented homes for their families around Gympie, I'm not exactly sure where in the township.

The world was in a terrible financial slump. Countries were not able to pay their way and then the bottom fell out of everything, and my father lost heavily in Assurance Investments, but we were able to cover our daily debts. Worse still, in 1929, the whole work force of the P.M.G. in Australia was stood down, only keeping on a skeleton staff to keep the mail and telephone service running.

Unfortunately, my dad and his two mates weren't part of the remaining staff. Men were desperate at not being able to pay their rents so my dad helped out his two mates.

The three families held a meeting at Dad and Mum's home and Dad suggested that they build a poultry farm. He had noticed a 40acre property on the corner of Old Maryborough Road and Parsons Road backing onto the unformed Tucker Street with an old, two storey Queenslander home facing Tucker Street which they all could share. Dad bought it by Miner's Lease. All three families and their six children moved in, with the Young and Stark families upstairs and the Stokes family downstairs.

Dad had his rugby car cut down to a utility by Jacky Smith, the coach and body builder in Monkland Street and Dad used it to collect rough bush timber from a gentleman living in a tent on the corner of Old Maryborough Rd and Hamilton Rd. At that time Old Maryborough Road was a two-wheel track with the trees meeting over the road.

I was born in the nursing home up on Channon Street in May 1930, making a total of six adults and seven young children living in the Tucker Street home for about 5-6 years.

The three families worked hard to build the chook runs and feeding bins. I can still see the shed that held two egg incubators. One took 80 eggs and the other one 120 eggs. (The 80-egg incubator is at present (2022) in the Gympie & District Historical Museum at Monkland). Dad approached the newly started Egg Marketing Board in Roma Street Brisbane re: supplying eggs, costs etc.

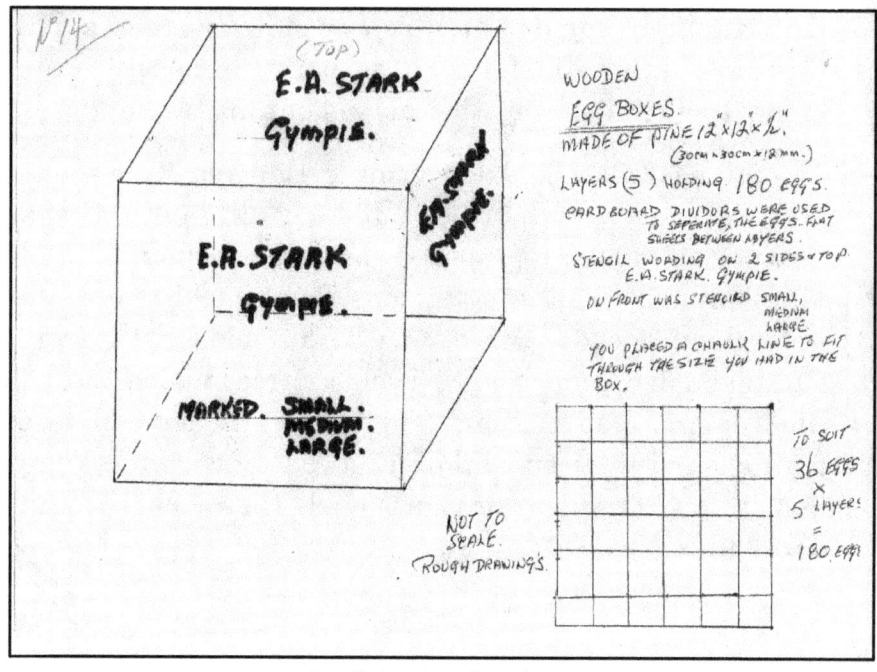

Rough drawing of egg boxes.

I can still see Mr. Young making the boxes to freight the eggs to Brisbane, cutting the flat pine sheets into squares 12" x 12" x ½" thick, nailing the ends, sides and bottom together. When full with 180 eggs he would nail on the lid. All boxes would have the stencil E.A. Stark, Gympie, stamped on the lid and two sides to allow the empty boxes be returned to the Gympie Railway Goods Shed. I watched my dad loading dozens of these boxes into the Ute and I sometimes went with him and watched while he unloaded them onto the bag trolley and wheel them into the Goods shed.

At this time the Railway Goods Shed had seven carriers registered to deliver all the goods to the customers. I remember Mr. Hood, with his Chevy tray back and Mr Thomas, with his two beautiful chestnut Clydesdale horses harnessed to a four-wheel flat top wagon (his mode of delivery). Mr. Thomas continued his carrying business until the mid-1970s when he retired to his home in Queen Street.

About the end of 1929, all things were running smoothly, it was decided that with Mr. Stokes and the ladies running between 2000 and 3000 laying hens, Mr. Young and my dad seemed to have very little to do. After a discussion together, they came up with the idea, that since bread was delivered by horse and cart from Branch's Bakery, they wondered if Mr Branch would sell them bread and buns to deliver to their own customers. Dad approached Mr. Branch who seemed a little set back, because there had never been a buyer of bread before, only horse and cart deliveries by the bakehouse. Dad realised that if he was successful, it would be a draw on one bakehouse so he also approached Mr. Tom Condie with the same proposition, but he said no. He and Dad couldn't come to an agreement mainly due to the price structure. He then spoke to Mr. Bradford at his bakery in Red Hill Road and he also agreed, not thinking that it would come to anything. Dad bought another tourer, a Chevrolet 1926 model, with very little use and had it remade into a utility. Mr. Young and my dad then started to canvas the area close to Horseshoe Bend, and with wonderful results, set a starting date a month away.

They had 2 bread boxes also made by Mr. Smith. They were all surprised at the result, so they decided to call themselves "Bread Vendors". The first in Queensland.

On Easter Friday, the Branch's made and baked Hot Cross Buns only for my dad. They were delivered hot to all the customers who had placed orders with my dad and Mr Young. The carters delivered Easter buns on their Wednesday runs, as they always had Thursdays off. This covered their working on Saturdays and attending to their horses and equipment.

I went to the bakery quite often, watching the bakers handling the bread dough, never thinking that 10 years later, I would be operating brick oven N°2 (with Billy Branch as my offsider). Billy was the carter in the photo taken by Murray's of Mary Street in 1930.

Branch's Bakery- Photo 1930

This photo shows Dad dressed in his 'best' clothes with a hat, tie, and hand knitted vest. He looked the part of an engineer standing beside his 1926 Rugby utility and the Branch family and staff. To my knowledge no photo was ever taken of Mr. Young and his utility.

Back at the poultry farm things were very busy, mother had to find extra help and engaged Mrs. Dollan of Rifle Range Road. Eggs were bringing 1/9d (17c) a dozen at the Egg Board and with Dad working as a bread vendor as well, things were going splendidly. At my dad's funeral we discovered his generosity to the customers that he knew did not have any way of paying their accounts.

I can remember thousands of men on the move by foot, seeking any kind of work across Australia. A ration was granted by the federal government of a portion of flour, salt, and tea, all available at police stations. The Gympie police station in Channon Street handed out the rations but to get their next ration of food the men would have to move up to Maryborough. Many hopped onto the goods trains – highly illegal.

In Gympie, if they were caught by the railway cop, Mr. Bill Connellan (aka Wingie), it meant three days in Gympie Watchhouse — time to wash dirty clothes, have hot food and a dry bed at night. I personally knew Mr. Connellan from his association with my dad. He had lost his left arm and acquired his nickname in an accident with a tiger moth airplane at Cairns.

At night, I would see up to 150 men of all ages pulling long grass to make a bed in the covered pig and calf pens allowing them some protection from the cold, harsh nights.

Then, people walked everywhere. Only once during a bad storm, do I remember dad come and pick us up. We were about a third of the way home under the awning of the Northumberland Hotel.

My sisters and I attended the Methodist Church at Red Hill and walked to Sunday School. Dad and Mum decided that it would be a shorter walk for us if we attended Surface Hill Methodist Church, so Dad and Mum changed their membership.

In 1933 Dad sold the Parsons Road property to Mr. and Mrs. Ferris Snr, from the Southside dairy property and the Ferris' built a lovely Queenslander on the corner of Tucker Street and Parsons Road. Later on, the Ferris' and the church hierarchy subdivided the rest of the acreage for houses and a Methodist Church.

Over the next few years, the economy slowly improved. It was a lovely surprise when a letter arrived for dad from the P.M.G. stating that, as of the 17th August 1937, all staff would be reinstated to their previous positions. Dad approached Mr. Branch with this letter and he agreed to buy the two delivery runs from dad. Mr. Branch replaced Harry Young's run with a horse and cart driven by Mr. Norm Ganley. Dad's run was divided between the rest of the carters.

Dad kept the two utilities for about 18 months, and they were eventually sold to Roy and Viv Cassidy Garages who had previously done all the servicing on the vehicles. The bread boxes were still under Mum and Dads' home when they sold it to Mr and Mrs. McKay in 1953.

These high poles, which my dad used to climb, had at least nine to eighteen cross arms with clear and white glass cups along each arm. They were about sixty feet apart, and left the Gympie railway station yards, went down Mellor Street, right into Fern Street, up Nash Street, left into Channon Street to the P.M.G. exchange on the corner of Channon and Duke Streets, where the exchange girls would ask you "number please".

My dad's office was a tin shed with a dirt floor behind the Post Office. At one end of the shed about one hundred batteries were stored to give two amps of power which was enough to run these telephone lines.

Can you imagine an engineer today working under these conditions? He had to travel everywhere by train and did not receive a vehicle till after the end of the Second World War! His working territory covered from Caboolture in the south to Miriam Vale in the north. Dad had many parties (teams) of men working on lines and exchange connections.

William John Pritchard (John) came to Gympie with his wife, Irene, and baby daughter, Rosalyn, on the 26th July 1930, from his parent's (William and Sarah) property at Lacey's Creek via Dayboro. The depression was digging too deep for their farm to carry two sons and their families.

This pole situated in the Gympie Railway yards are similar to ones of my youth.

Irene's father, Fritz Rospigaroff, was a master builder. With the drop-off of work in the building industry he and his wife, Laura, decided to purchase a large dairy property at Wilsons Pocket, between Gympie and Tin Can Bay.

They offered the helping hand of half share farming to their daughter and son-in-law John, thus

William John Pritchard. Photo 1919

allowing Fritz to engage in local building. Over the next 20 years, Fritz worked on the extensions to the Goomboorian Hall, plus many new homes.

John Pritchard loading hay on the farm. Photo 1935

John stayed on the farm for 6 years but being a timber man in Lacey's Creek (where he had his own bullock team), he felt he could do better for his family if he got back into that industry. He moved his family into a little cottage at 3 Rose Street, Gympie. It was far too small for a family with 3 young children (Rosalyn, Ronald, and baby June), but the depression was on, and you took what you could and made do.

Work was still practically non-existent, so John applied to the Gympie City Council to work on the two day a week relief scheme for married men and was put on the gang of workers building the Surface Hill Methodist Church stone wall and the stone walls in Young Street.

Stone wall, Surface Hill Methodist Church. Photo 1990

He found a slightly larger home at 38 King Street, owned by Miss Thelma Kluver, and backing Kate Russell and her dad's closed bakehouse in Iron Street. They lived there for about 4years. In 1942 the Pritchard's moved into 7 Iron Street.

Mr & Mrs Rospigaroff sold the dairy property at Wilson's Pocket to Mr. Len Stephen and his family. Len later became our State Member of Parliament for many years.

In 1937 he found timber work with Peter Rasspinson and when the 2nd World War finished, he bought a K5 International truck from Army Disposal and had Jacky Smith make a trailer. From then on, he obtained plenty of work.

Ron Pritchard with K45 International Truck – Photo 1946

Mr. Pritchard used to call into Harry's Bakery each Monday morning to pick up bread supplies for his timber cutters who were working in the mountains around Kilkivan. Bread was only 4d (pence) for a two-pound loaf which is the equivalent to 3 cents for 1kg loaf in today's decimal. Mr. Pritchard would pay 3 shillings and tuppence (3/2d) for 8 loaves = 32cents today.

He would also pay Mrs. Cox, who owned the General Store next door to the bakery, the sum of £1.00($2) a week for the rent of their home in Iron Street. I did not know that in a few years' time I would court and, on the 20th

January, 1951, marry Mr. & Mrs. Pritchard's beautiful eldest daughter Rosalyn.

7 Iron Street, Gympie 1952

In 1947 they purchased this home from Mrs. Cox, raised their 6 children there and only sold it in the 1990s, when Irene Pritchard moved into full-time care at Cooinda Nursing Home. Irene passed away in 2002, John had previously passed away in 1978.

I understand that Mrs. Cox owned about 26 homes in this area of Gympie. I knew the Cox family very well as they also belonged to the Surface Hill Methodist Church.

I remember going with Dad to Mrs. McDonald's Store on the South Side. At that time all that was out there was The Jockey Club Hotel, Showgrounds, South Side School, and the Ferris family dairy farm and a very stony, dirt road to Glastonbury. I wondered back then where Mrs. McDonald would receive her trade from and what Dad would have to charge her for the bread he was delivering and what she would retail it to her customers for. Today in 2020 that shop still stands and is three times larger than the original.

As the photo shows it is still a thriving business. Of course, now there are houses as far as the eye can see.

For four years during the war, we had up to 6000 infantrymen stationed at the Gympie Showgrounds, and in areas around Gympie, for training and all were camping in tents. The army had its own Bakehouse kitchen and supplied food to all its units in Gympie.

In 1948, when I enlisted in the Army, I never told them that I was a Baker. I wanted to stay with my mates in Infantry.

McDonalds Store. Photo 2018

My bakehouse career from 1944 to 1969 ranges from making hand-made doughs for bread and cakes, using wax candles and from oven lights that ran on dripping, to kerosene, then Direct Current (DC) and finally Alternating Current (AC) power. The ovens ranged from internal wood fires, to side wood firing, to oil fired brick ovens of all sizes. Over the years of my bakery career, I owned two bakeries and worked as a Master Baker and Pastry Chef at quite a few more and also worked with the Bread Master Bakers Association of Queensland as a relieving Master Baker and travelling with my family all over Queensland working in large and small towns so the resident baker could take a well-earned holiday for a month.

I thank the manufacturers of all the new machinery that made our work so much easier. Doughmaking, Bread Rolling, Cakemaking, Pastry Rolling Machines, Oil and electric fired brick and steel ovens.

Thank you for your precious time. Enjoy and live with me my stories of The Old Bakehouses and Families of Gympie.

Author

Chapter 1
"William Thomas Weller".
The Bakehouse at Widgee Crossing.
1867-1868

William Weller Snr.

The first verbally recorded bakehouse in this area was made of rough pole timber, dirt floor, bark roof, two push-out windows and an opening for a door. He would have also had a good size tent and a wagon drawn by a couple of horses which would have carried their possessions and the ingredients for making bread.

When William Weller with his young wife and two small boys, Thomas and William jnr. joined the movement of men from Nanango, setting out for the gold strike of Black Snake, Kilkivan, he had no idea what lay ahead for them. He had spent 12 months working for the baker in Nanango and previous to that, two years in a bakery in Brisbane. He set off, hoping that he could supply the vast hordes with bread, but when he arrived at Kilkivan, the movement of men had already begun to leave this 12-month-old goldfield for the new strike at Nashville on the Mary River. He had been told by the acting Commissioner on site, that anyone could peg out a claim at Nashville and pick up the gold with your hands, so they decided to set out in that direction.

A track had to be made through the thick scrub from Kilkivan through the area now known as Widgee and Glastonbury and on to Nashville. This would have created many problems for horse drawn wagons. The weather was against them too with late summer rain, but this did not deter them. They were told of the already named Widgee Crossing where they would be able to cross the Mary River.

As early as the 1820's men came from Andrew Petrie's sheep and cattle property in Parramatta, New South Wales. Men such as David Green and his son David, had explored and crisscrossed these lands, as far north as to what is called Mundubbera country, looking for open grass lands for feeding sheep and cattle. Land that was heavily timbered meant that too much work had to be done clearing the land before the animals could graze.

David's diaries were kept up to date with all the writings of their trips clearly marked. Their reports of the landscape are wonderful to read. I have been fortunate enough to read some of their reports written in indelible pencil (which could write under all conditions).

I was given the opportunity to privately view and read these original diaries of David Green Snr, a great, great grandfather to Gympie resident Mr. Brett Green.

Brett, is a published author of the local Aboriginal tribes-people and a great friend of mine.*

William and his family finally arrived at the crossing only to find the river in high flood. You can imagine the confusion of men, horses, and carts of all description when they saw the height of the flood water and realized they would be forced to remain here while the river went back down.

William saw his chance! While he was in Kilkivan, he had noticed a damaged ship water tank that he could change into an oven with a little bit of help from a blacksmith who was also stuck on the river bank. He sent word back to Kilkivan for men to hurriedly forward the tank to him and as many bags of flour as they could buy. He also tried to replenish his potatoes and corn (the ingredients of baker's yeast), but was told none was available. They would have to come from Nanango, and with this weather, it would probably take months.

The miners were wet and hungry. They usually carried a little flour and salt and made Duff loaves in their quart pots (a duff loaf was a sort of pudding they cooked in a cloth bag), a prelude to Damper.

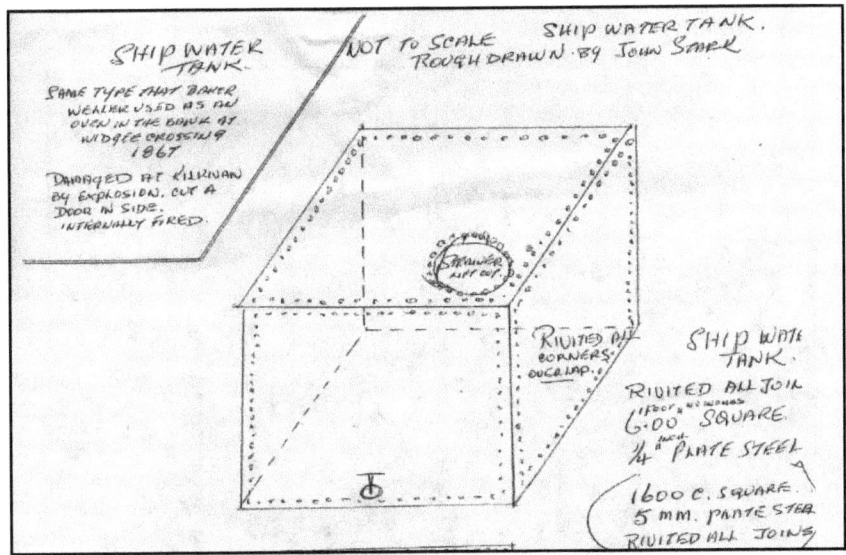

Rough drawing of a ship Water Tank

After the ship water tank arrived, William had the blacksmith cut a doorway into the tank and close off the water entrance to make a steel damper to control the internal fire *all bread ovens in those days were internally fired*. The piece of steel he removed he made into a swing door. He then buried the steel tank into the dirt bank.

Having no yeast, he handmade enough dough to make around 40 cob loaves (Dampers). That would be about the number to cover the floor of his new made oven.

The pole bakehouse with its bark roof, did not hold out well against the bad weather. A dirt floor and flour were not a good mix either.

There was no cut, dry timber for William Weller. During the day his helpers would have had to cut and collect stacks of wood. *Dead, if possible, as green wood gives off too much gas and it would be practically impossible to cook with such heat*. The timber would have been soaked wet in the rain, they would have had to find or build some sort of coverage for the timber too.

I felt for all those families! Boy! They would have been busy all day to produce enough dampers to feed all those who were held up at the crossing.

Widgee Crossing Road. - 2020

This road is still in the same place in 2020 and has not been changed since William Weller and thousands of men travelled down it in the 1800s. Those days there was a third track in the centre made by the horses towing the wagons.

Easter of 1938. As boy scouts & cubs we came down to camp at Widgee Crossing. The high ground as you can see, came down to a flat clear ground on the right.

If you carry on down these tracks, you can see Mr. John Colls standing in the original dug out road to the river.

Three generations of John Colls' family have occupied the 120 acres of land on the right side of this road as you come in and 480 acres of heavy timbered land up opposite the now Glastonbury Road as a dry paddock for their pregnant dairy cows. Today, John and his family still live on the 18 acres running down to the Mary River.

John Colls standing where William Weller had his makeshift bakery on the bank of Mary River. - 2020

*The Runge Brothers, Billy, Irvine, and John, mining engineers, built a bridge just upriver from the old crossing in 1950. This made the way for the Runge boys to have their trucks remove the river sand and be easily transported to their Gympie treatment works for the removal of Gold. Sadly, John was killed on the 4.02.1952 when the front-end loader he was driving rolled over in soft sand on the Gympie side of Mary River.

*Old road marked leading down to Mary River.
Unable to reach the river or site of Runge Bridge. - 2020*

This bridge was used by all the people who lived in the surrounding area and was swept away in the Great Flood of 1955. The treatment works company, together with the local Widgee Shire Council, did not replace the bridge and only a odd few posts still remain, leaning westward, from all the floods since its destruction*.

*Oak was always used by bakers back in the old home country. In Australia, there was a similar oak tree that serviced all wood firing equipment up until 1945 when it became impossible for the timber cutters to find any left in our forests. From then on, every one obtained a mixture of forest timbers. Bakers, along with the Hospitals, were supplied with forest wood of all sorts, and when dried made a reasonable fire.

One of the timber cutters was Mr. Brady Snr from Corella, who had property on Brady Flats on Old Maryborough Road. This land was the overnight stop for all the horses and wagons coming from Maryborough. An early start next morning would see the wagons arriving in Gympie and delivering goods to all customers early in the day.

Grandad Brady's son, Eric, was my age. I can see them both in our horse paddock in Clematis Street, stacking up the wood delivery. They started supplying Gympie Bakeries in 1870. His sons carried on the business until 1972. The Brady's were always very busy and kept well ahead with stocks of stacked cordwood. Cords were 30feet long x 4feet wide and stacked 5feet high. The same was supplied to mines, hospitals, shipyards, and railways. Private homes had smaller versions.

At the bakehouses we had at least had five cords ahead to allow the sap to dry. The last job for the day was to bring the wood from outside into the wood boxes in the bakery. If it was soaked with the rain, we filled the fire boxes - they sure dried out quick. We also threw a few sheets of iron over the cords in the horse paddock, that helped a lot too*.

When I retired back to Gympie in 1983, Rosalyn and I bought a portion of the Brady cattle property, and we were neighbours to Eric and June until we sold the property for Rosalyn and I to move into the Palmwoods Retirement Village in 2013. We would have preferred to stay in Gympie, but the town didn't have any married aged care facilities at that time. Eric lost his wife in 2015 and I lost my Rosalyn in 2017.

Now take time to think, the river was in flood, water full of mud, so what did those loaves taste like — a little muddied I would think, but hunger is a wonderful changer of the taste of foods. William had to haul the water all the way up to the bake house in buckets. I suppose he had plenty of helpers — men with time on their hands.

The floods showed no mercy, they rose and fell for about eight months, by this time there was a tent city and, finally in the spring, they found the river was low enough to be able to be crossed.

You can imagine the rush of many people, as the cry went out that Joe Jones had crossed the river to the other side, with his sulky loaded up with all his belongings.

Everybody, probably in their hundreds, all queuing to go down that one track as shown in the photos, to escape the trap that the swollen river had been.

William pulled up stakes, joined the convoy, and moved into Nashville.

CHAPTER 2

The bakehouse of William Thomas Weller
Blocks 179, 181, 183, Nashville
1868-1879

*It would have taken days to move everyone to the Nashville side of the river. I would say that William would have made contact with friends to have reserved some special blocks in the heart of the workings.

I am also sure that he would have pulled out his manufactured steel oven, left behind his log shop, and progressed to this special block at 179 Nashville – out of reach of flood waters. The Assistant Commissioner would have recorded the block on this busy dirt track. In the future, this track became known as Brisbane Road.

I would say that William would have employed a wagon and horses to move his ship tank oven from Widgee Crossing to the new property. Then he set up his oven beside the road. While travelling, all his doughs were made in a big tin bath*.

Anything of any size and weight could only be moved by teams of either bullocks or horses. In 1890, the 2 South Great Eastern Mine ordered a new Colonial Boiler 30 feet(ft) (9.1m) long. It travelled from Maryborough by steam train and arrived at Gympie Station, then was moved to Monkland by wagon and a team of 16 draft horses. The photo is in the Gympie Historical Museum.

Luck was on William's side as he set up his tank oven on block 179. Even without the dirt bank to help hold the heat in, the steel of the tank was so thick he managed to produce dampers and once he could make yeast, he finally produced bread.

There was already a brick maker and builder on the goldfield. A supply of clay mud was found at Long's Gully just to the north of the field, now called Tamaree. There was no way of baking the handmade bricks so they had to dry in the sun for a week.

In 1868 William Weller built their bakery exactly where the double lines are in 2020.

They were built into the bread oven the next. William told him how to make a brick oven. The walls were 14" (35.5cm) thick, which was the normal thickness back then. The newly made bricks just stuck together, the arched hood of the oven was bonded by the first firing, very slow and light, allowing the bricks to harden. This was done over a few days.

William now had plenty of flour and a supply of corn and potatoes to make yeast and was finally able to produce bread. It surprised him how well these handmade bricks stood up to the heavy wear of an internal fire and cleaning.

After the railway from Maryborough was finished in 1871, William could then be supplied with kiln dried bricks by train. William must have sung for joy when bread tins arrived, and the new oven was finished. This oven could hold and cook 180 x 900g loaves. A cob damper cost 2d (1c) and a 2lb (900g) loaf of bread cost 3d (2c). A 1lb (450g) loaf cost 1½d (2c).

*In Queensland, bread prices increased in increments of 1 farthing (1 quarter of 1 penny) right up to 1972. Farthings

haven't been used as coinage since 1914. I have one in my coin collection.

Wages those days for a 48 hour plus, no overtime, no unions either, was £2 ($4). If you operated an oven, with all the responsibility of firing, cooking, and cleaning the oven, you received an extra 5/- (50c).

And boy! the trouble you were in if you burnt any bread or cakes. Those days it was hard yakka!*.

The boys William and Thomas were now young men.

William Thomas & Thomas William Weller

Thomas followed his father into the baking business, and they branched into handmade pies and pasties, followed by cakes, a luxury for the men who were hard rock miners.

His brother, William Jnr, decided he would become a butcher.

I am sure William Thomas Weller snr. would have liked his two sons to follow his trade, but Bakers & Butchers are good trades to follow and go together like hands in gloves.

With all that was going on in Gympie, it would have been hard to obtain trade persons, even if they were nearby. They were all there to find gold, not to work with timber, bricks, and mortar. Everything in 1869 would have been built in a very rough state. At the Gympie Historical Museum, you can see a typical hut with slab walls and floors. Though the hut, when being lived in on the goldfields, would probably have had a bark roof.

William snr. built a cottage next to the bakehouse with slab timber walls and floors. In 1878 he replaced the slab hut with a two-bedroom weatherboard home.

One morning in 1879, while he was working in the bakehouse, William's wife came in and told him he had three visitors from the Government who informed him that the new railway line was being built from Brisbane to Gympie, and according to the drawn plans, the line would run right through his bakery.

When the shock finally settled, he asked how long did he have to move his home and bakehouse? The Government men expected that the line would come through Monkland and on to Gympie some time in 1881. They then stated they were authorized to offer a payment that would suffice both parties. The cream came a few weeks later, when they offered William a wonderful sum to buy his home and they would move it to the left side of the new line to become the Gatekeeper's house.

During the war, thousands of convoys, troop and munition trains came up to cross the road at these railway gates. The gate

My 1946 Royal Enfield. Photo 1948

keeper and the staff of the nearby Monkland Station were on call 24 hours a day. When the war began in 1939, the gate keeper became a job for the ladies and stayed this way till lights were installed at this crossing.

I was on my new 1946 Royal Enfield motorbike and I can remember this little lady coming out to swing open those old heavy wooden gates. The little home was removed in the 1970's.

The Railway opened the Brisbane to Gympie line in 1881. A PB15 shunter steam engine was always stationed at Monkland and used for every goods train that came to Gympie from Brisbane because of the lift of 110' (33.5m) from Monkland Station to the Gympie Station platform. The shunter would not hook onto the train, just come up from behind and push it up the long, steep grade. Then, it would just reverse down the line to Monkland to do it all over again for the next goods train*.

After waiting for over 12 months, it was with relief and excitement Mr. Wellers' new dough making trough (spelt trough, but pronounced tro), arrived by train from Maryborough. This trough was lined with a new metal called Zincanneal. Now, when making the doughs they had to use a scraper, instead of a knife.

I personally worked with many Zincanneal troughs over 12' (3.5m) long, width 2'6" (800mm) and depth of 2'3" (700mm)*.

*The wooden troughs that they first mixed the doughs in were made using one slab of pine for each side, end, and base.

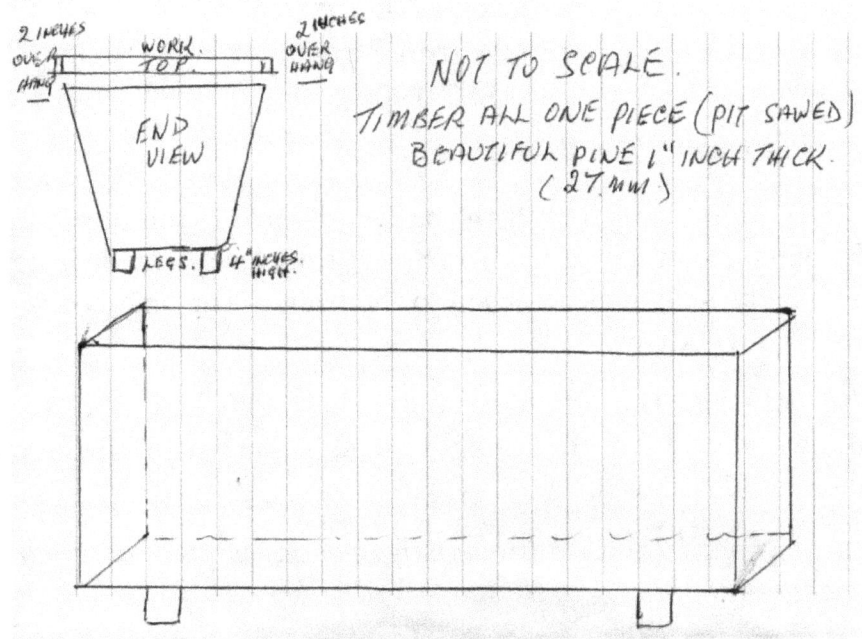

Rough Drawing of Wooden Trough

*Also, it was rumoured, that in England, some big company, had invented a dough making machine that connected to a stationary steam engine and was driven by a leather belt — no hands, what was the world coming to.

Many stories were told to me by Abe Doss, his story comes in Chapter 4 — Longs bakery*.

Chapter 3

Russell's Bakery
42-42a Iron Street
1887-1909

As told to me by Ted Priddy.

In 1887, John Russell built the bakehouse at 42 Iron Street and a 2-bedroom cottage at 42a Iron Street from locally made bricks. The baker's shop was attached to the front of the bakehouse by a covered walkway.

John only had the one oven and it held 220 loaves. He had baking tins to take 4lb (1.8kg) of dough, known to all the old bakers as Tin loaves.

I never heard Ted Priddy ever speak of any cartage of bread to the general public.

In 2002, Rosalyn and I went to the Gayndah Orange Festival, we walked into the old bakery still in operation and with a three-quarter dividing wall between the bakery and the shop and I asked for a Tin loaf. The young lady looked puzzled, but out of the bakery came a voice, "that must be a bloody old bloke!" We all had a good laugh. I was 72-odd years old then.

John and Eliza Russell had 2 children, John jnr. and Catherine, a redhead with a spirit to match.

Ted Priddy and Catherine grew up as near neighbours and walked to Central School together.

John snr. closed down his business and retired in 1909 due to ill health. Hand making doughs was just too hard on his body.

John jnr. did not want to be a baker but he loved selling groceries. At 14yrs old, he obtained a position working for Thurecht Brothers, Grocers at 202 Mary Street, John jnr. spent his whole working life with Thurechts.

The Thurechts, Coxs, Russells, Condies, Cosiers, and Starks all belonged to the Surface Hill Methodist Church in Channon

Street. Word of mouth was all that was required to obtain positions in those days.

John Russell snr. passed away 29.08.1930.

I remember calling in to see Cate in 1945. She was still living in the little brick home, having never married. The bakehouse had been destroyed. Kate showed me what was left. When they destroyed the bakehouse, they left 4' (1.22m) of the outside wall of the old oven, to make the back boundary.

Cate looked after her mother, Eliza, until she passed on 10.10.1967. Cate lived until 30.05.1979. The family is buried in the 2-mile Cemetery at Gympie.

John jnr. courted and married Elizabeth Cavanaugh.

*I knew Mrs Russell all my life, to my knowledge she was always President of the Ladies Guild of Surface Hill Church. She chastised us boys when we ran through the Sunday School Hall. All the crockery would rattle in the wooden stand in the kitchen section.

Mr and Mrs Russell had one son, Ivan. At 14 he started working with his father at Thurechts. After 2 years, Mrs. Cox offered him a better position at her store at 70 Duke St.

In 1962, visiting Rosalyn's parents with our 4 young children, I called in to Eric Heilbronn's store in Duke St to pick up some cold meat and decided to see if Mrs Russell was still alive in Barter Street. The home had not changed at all, the wooden lattice privacy screen on the front verandah was still in place. I knocked and when Mrs Russell saw me, she burst into tears and hugged me. She was so pleased to see 'one of her boys'.

Quite a few months later I was told that she had passed away. There are no records of hers or her husband John jnrs'. burial in any of Gympie's cemetery records.

Ivan Russell was 8 years older than I. In the church, his friends were Merv Griffiths, Viv and Reg Hayes, Bob Sexton, and Bill Collins. My group of friends used to say Goodday as we passed them by. We were not in their league for tennis, cricket, or any sport.

Ivan enlisted into the army in 1939 and saw service in Egypt, Libya, and the Pacific. Because the Government had made a law that all staff who had joined the Australian forces had to be re-employed in their previous position when he returned home in 1946, he called into Harry's bakery and stated that he was soon to take over as manager of Cox's General Store.

Ivan courted and married Kath Cosier of Jane St who also belonged to our church in 1949. They bought Mrs. Sax's home at 62 Duke Street and a few years later had it demolished and replaced it with a new home in the same style as the home Rosalyn and I had built in 2 Iron Street in 1953.

He worked with Mrs. Cox until she closed the store in 1957.

Ivan and Kath then bought the Gift store at 75 Mary Street which served Gympie until 1981 when they sold out.

Ivan developed cancer in the face and passed away in 1983. I visited him at his home in Duke Street only a few days before his passing*. There aren't any records of Ivan's internment in Gympie Cemeteries either.

My wife Rosalyn knew Cate well when Rosalyn was a young girl. When Rosalyn's parents moved into town in 1937, the house in this photo is the home that backed on to Cate's fence and Rosalyn remembered the old brick wall, where she and her brother Ron often sat before their family moved into their own home at 7 Iron Street.

Rosalyn, June, Ron Pritchard Photo 1937

I looked when I took the recent photo, but the brick wall was gone.

Strange coincidence! Rosalyn's first shop – Dress Designer and Seamstress was at 220 Mary Street. Her second shop was at 202 Mary Street – originally Thurect Bros Grocery Store.

*Recently, when I was taking the photo of where John Russell's old bakery stood, now having two houses built in the 1980's on the property, the owner of property No: 42A came out and asked, "what was I up to taking a photo of her home?" I explained what I was there for, and I asked her if she ever wondered why her home number was 42A.

She stated that it never crossed her mind, so I told her the Russell story. Afterwards she just shrugged her shoulders and walked inside*.

42, 42a Iron Street. Photo 18/04/2018

Chapter 4

Henry Long, Baker
72-74 Duke Street
1883-1936

It was in the early months of 1883 when a young baker named Henry Long thought that another bakery in the fast-growing town, now known as Gympie, would be in order. He travelled by steamer to the ever-expanding port of Tewantin with the main implements (that he purchased in Brisbane) to equip a new bakery. He then bought a dray and two horses and travelled overland to Gympie.

The Assistant Gold Commissioner told Henry the type of land he required could be found on high ground, at Blocks 72 - 74 Duke Street. Henry arranged for a small two-bedroom home to be built on block 74 for his wife Alma and two young sons.

Henry Longs 2nd home built in 1922 over the existing house. Photo 2018

A compound called cement, brought from England in the holds of ships to give stability in sailing, had made its way to the goldfield. Henry employed a bricklayer to build a cement tank at the rear of this new home, it was approximately 10' (3m) across, 9' (2.7m) deep and set 6'6" (1.98m) into the ground allowing 3' (.9m) above ground. This tank filled quickly with rainwater from the cottage roof, allowing them to build the bakery and have water for bread when the first oven was completed.

The bakery was built from Gympie supplies. Double thick brick with the new cement, with one push out window 3' (90cm) wide x 2'6" (79cm) high on the house side and a wood entrance window 18" (45.7cm) wide x 5' (152cm) high next to the right-hand corner face of the oven. This window allowed the bakers to load the wood into the wood box inside the bakery. Henry also had a fireplace built into the house side wall of the bakery below the oven floor level, so the dough-maker could boil up potatoes and corn, to make yeast for the bread.

Gympie was declared a city in 1905.

*Ted Priddy told me that, on occasions, Henry would find the dough maker "under the weather". This mixture had a strong alcoholic content, and the dough maker would take a sip out of the dipper as he handmade the doughs. Making doughs was a big, hot, dry job and it took two and a half hours to make one eight-hour dough.

I know, I used to take my turn as dough maker at Harry's Bakery when Stan Blakeway went on holidays and I had to make three big doughs of 300 loaves each - 1x 8 hour, 1x 6 hour and 1x 4 hour. The difference in time for the doughs was controlled by how much yeast you used.

Showing placement of bakery, home, and Mrs. Cox's shop

I have drawn in the position of the bakehouse. This home was built in 1922 and was the second home that Henry had built on Block 74. Open verandahs right across the front of the house, down the right side and across the back to the kitchen. Green wooden blinds closed in the verandah from the kitchen back to the front right corner.

The flour was stored under the house in 170-pound (lb) (77kg) bags. Big problem! the house should have been built 6" (15cm) higher. When we carried a bag of flour from under the house, we were caught by the floor plate, and it would whisk the bag of flour off your shoulder. Experienced bakers would bend down with the heavy bag and move outside easily. We apprentices would crumble at the knees.

When I first started doughmaking at 16 years of age, I would have to carry eight bags of flour and put each one onto the work bench inside the bakery. After I lifted each bag onto my shoulder, I would wobble all over the place until I got it balanced properly*.

Henry's staff at Duke Street were Abe Doss (who had told Bill's baker friend about the sale of Henry's bakery). Abe lived at 54 Duke Street and was employed as Henry's dough man. Ted Priddy lived at 4 Pine Street, and he was the No 1 oven man. Allan Reichlag was Ted's Jobber (baker off sider). No 2 ovens man was Henry. Allan Chapple was Henry's Jobber.

Henry employed two horse and cart carters to service all the customers he canvassed in the expanding town of Gympie. After two years of business, he had another oven built. The centre wall was removed, and he found that there was a difference between the two floor levels and a gap of 12" (30cm) in the floor, so he had a rise of 6 inches sloped into the doorway.

You always had to remember to raise your feet, or you would fall flat on your face.

The bakers last job for the day, was to bring in the wood from the horse paddock on a special trolley. Henry had it made with one wheel, two handles going back 5' (1.2m) with steel legs bolted to the two shafts which were bent to make the legs (like a wheelbarrow frame). You then loaded the 4' (1.22cm) long timber, to the amount you thought you could balance, and head up to the bakehouse wood box window.

Sometimes you made it and sometimes you didn't!!

When you were sure you had enough timber brought in, you would come inside and carry the wood across the front of the old oven and store it in the wood box for the new oven which Henry had called no 1.

In the 1890s Henry had two apprentices, Ted Priddy (14),

Ted Priddy's home, Pine Street. Built 1898. Photo 2021

Steve Heilbronn's Home, Pine Street. Photo 2021

Henry's jobber on Oven #1 and Steve Heilbronn (14), James Bradford's jobber on oven #2. Each apprentice had the job of looking after the wood supply to their oven.

Remember, the ovens had internal fires, when the baker responsible for that oven thought his oven was hot enough, he used a steel scraper 10' (3m) long and would drag the burning wood out onto the floor. He would then throw into the oven a handful of flour to check the temperature. If it only smouldered, the oven was too cold. If it exploded, the oven was too hot. When the flour was slow to combust, the baker was happy with it and he and the apprentice would take the fire out through the door to the front yard and throw water over it to put it out — not too much, as water was scarce.

As I have told you in Wellers' chapter the responsibility for the oven was all on the oven baker's head. If the oven was too hot, you then used a long pole with a bag tied on the end, you would dip the bag in water, open the door and by using a sweeping action you would cover the floor with water, thus cooling the brick oven floor, if still too hot you would continue to swab the oven till the right temperature, the good old flour thrown across the floor of the oven always gave you the right answer.

There was no such thing as a heat thermometer built into the front wall of the oven, that came many years later. Henry employed many bakers over the years. Abe Doss stayed most of his working life with Henry as dough maker.

One day in early 1930, James Bradford's wife, (who was a friend of Mrs. Long) had brought his lunch over to the bakehouse and on visiting Mrs. Long went into labour and delivered their 4th son, Keith, in Long's front bedroom. Keith and I started school together 1935 and kept in touch with each other our whole lives. He passed away in August 2021.

All bakers lived in close proximity to their bakehouse, available at short notice if there was an emergency.

James and his family had their home in Clematis Street.

Steve Heilbronn, who loved horses, stepped out of the bakehouse, and became one of Henry Long's carters.

After Abe retired, he used to visit the bakehouse every couple of days, as he lived only 5 allotments away in Duke Street. Abe passed away in 1971.

Henry's two boys were only mentioned at odd times, and to my knowledge, not involved in the bakehouse. They married and moved away from Gympie. When World War 1 started in 1914, Ted told me that they had both enlisted*.

Henry sold the business to Bill Blakeway in 1935. There was never any mention of Henry after the sale of the bakery.

Chapter 5

William Weller and Son - Bakers of Distinction
Cnr of Brisbane & Geordie Roads, Monkland
1880-1909

With the money he received from the sale of his bakery at 179-183 Brisbane Rd in 1880, William bought the corner blocks of Brisbane and Geordie Roads. They built a beautiful Queenslander home, a new bakehouse, and the shop next door in Geordie Road. The two brick ovens, holding 300 loaves apiece, were built by Brickie and his son, William Thompson, the renowned oven builders. They built the ovens in all outlying towns and were close friends of my parents, Eldor and Alma Stark.

Wellers excelled themselves with the making and decorating of Wedding, Birthday, and Christmas cakes.

William Snr and son, Thomas, ran this bakery till 1908, when William's wife, Ivy, passed away. Thomas then ran the bakery for another 12 months before he decided to close up shop. There were no children who wished to carry on. William Snr passed away in 1927. Over the next few years Thomas had the bakehouse removed and lived on in the home till he passed away on the 31/10/1944.

5 generations of Weller Family

The home was rented till 1996 when it was sold for removal and shifted to the Kingaroy district.

*It was a sorry day that the Weller's beautiful home was removed to make way for other industries. *

*This combined photo shows the 5 generations. Top left corner is William

Weller snr. Front is his two sons Thomas and William. Back left is William Jnr's son Mervyn Weller, and his two children Leonard and Desley. Seated in front, is Desley's daughter Sarah Green.

Leonard became a Master Builder. Leonard and his wife Val live in Southside, Gympie. *

This corner is so busy today, as it is the junction of the Bruce Highway and the highway to Tin Can Bay and Rainbow Beach. The Tin Can Bay Highway is also the coast road to Maryborough.

Leonard Weller 2020

This spot is where we removed the tins and boots that were tied onto the back of our Morris z Utility. (All couples who left Gympie by car on their honeymoons did the same). The road south of Gympie which was known as the "road to Brisbane" was tarred to Monkland and only a dirt road south from there.

Rosalyn and I were on our way home from our honeymoon when we stopped and took the photo.

Tar was procured from the Gympie Gas works; this was the prelude of bitumen road surfaces.

End of bitumen Photo 1951

Dirt road to Chermside. Tar was used in "most" towns. Four hours of driving by car. Brisbane Road followed the railway line into and through all the small towns, plus all those railway gates where the road crossed the line, that had to be opened and closed. Just think, in 1870 it took 1½ days by Cobb and Co, with the overnight stop at Woombye*.

When Rosalyn's parents came to Gympie in 1930, Dayboro to Monkland. Gympie was 8 hours driving and all dirt road even in the towns. Her mother, nursing 10-day old Rosalyn, suffered with a very sore head from hitting the wooden roof spars. No seat belts those days.

Chapter 6

James Condie – Baker
32-38 Reef Street
1878-1884

William James Condie (known as James) was born and received his education in Cuden Fide, Dundee, Scotland, before travelling to Brisbane in 1861 where he married a lovely girl named Ruth who he met on the ship out to Australia. James and Ruth had two sons, Charles and Thomas.

James worked for a baker in Spring Hill for 12 years and decided to move to a town that showed prosperity. Gympie was their choice. Here, he worked for another baker for 12 months. *Unfortunately, the name of his employer wasn't recorded. Possibly could have been Wellers or Longs*.

In 1878, he purchased the mining leases at 34 and 36 Reef Street off another baker who had left Gympie before he finished building his premises.

Reef Street was named after all the newly found gold in reefs not far below the surface.

No name was recorded of the original owner of 34 and 36 Reef Street.

James had Brickie Thompson snr. finish the half-completed oven which was built over the dividing line of blocks 34 and 36. In the first 12 months of business, the Condies took up the blocks numbered 32 and 38 Reef Street, also the 4 blocks behind for slab timber stables and horse paddocks.

They had a builder construct a two-bedroom cottage of sawn timber on block 38. This became James and Ruth's home. Charles built on block 32 and Thomas built just round the corner, opposite the church in Channan Street. Both the boys completed their trade at the Reef Street bakery.

James had Brickie Thompson snr. build his second oven, which was made with a fire box built into the right side. This new oven was built to the right of oven $^{no}1$.

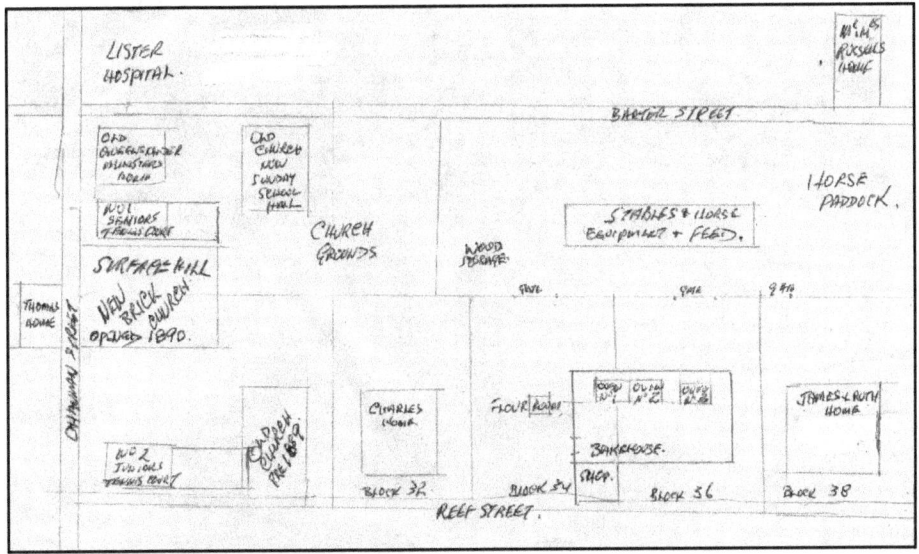

Mud map of Condies bakery and homes

X marks 32, 34 Reef St. Square marks the original flour room. Photo 2018

On block 36 the flour building had been built very close to the bakery, so it was moved diagonally backwards 12' (3.66m) to allow room for the horses and carts to go through to the stables and paddock at the rear of the bakery and for carters to load their bread deliveries each day.

In 1884 James suddenly died.

34 & 36 Reef St. X marks all that is left of the original bakery. Photo 2018

Chapter 7

W & J Condie – Bakers
32-38 Reef Street
1884-1952

After the funeral for James, Ruth and her eldest son, Charles, went into partnership together as W & J Condie.

Charles had obtained bulk sales for their bread. Maybe he had forward knowledge of the new type of bread tins with lids because he had already purchased the tins to suit the 2lb (900g) loaves, 12" (30cm) long x 4" (10cm) wide and the large 4lb (1.8kg) tins were 18" (45cm) x 6" (16cm) long. These new loaves were known as sandwich loaves.

Buyers of ordered sandwich loaves were delighted when the loaves came sliced ready to use. The bakery sold these loaves at 6d, double the price. The loaves were sliced by the new hand operated bacon cutter, newly arrived from England and sold to all the bakehouses by the wholesaler General Supply Store in Sydney.

Condies supplied bread for the local dances, the Gympie Hospital Board, and the Glandore Private Hospital. They also supplied the new Railway Refreshment Rooms. At this time Gympie had 46 Hotels and W & J Condie supplied them all.

The boys never let onto me how they came to supply and deliver by horse and cart such a wide portion of Gympie's trade.

*Charles married Emily and they had 4 boys. Thomas, Allen, Lesley, and Henry. Thomas was the only son who eventually married at the age of 56. They had no children.

Charles' brother, Thomas, married Ann and they had two girls, Jessie and Elizabeth, and a son, David, who loved mathematics and became an accountant. He moved to Brisbane where he met and married Ruth and had a son, Athol, who spent a lot of time with his grand-parents and Aunt Jessie in Gympie and became one of my childhood friends. Athol was a keen cricketer and played in our Church Cricket Team*.

When Rosalyn and I were married, I had the bakery at Amamoor. We left Gympie and I have never heard of, or seen, Athol again. Such a pity! I never thought to try and locate him in all the years we lived in Brisbane.

Church Cricket Team. Athol Condie arrowed.
Unfortunately, I was at work that day. Photo 1947

*The Baptist followers already had the lease of block 30 right through to Barter St, where the Surface Hill Church now stands and built a bark humpy called "The Bethel".

It is recorded that miners and their families were very religious. The Methodist Church which replaced "The Bethel" was packed for the 11am and the 7.30pm services every Sunday.

When my family attended Surface Hill, the Welsh miners had beautiful voices. The junior choir at the morning service was a delight to hear. But! the main choir at the night service was something amazing to listen to. my father was one of the top first tenors in this choir, I sang second tenor. I will tell you more about singing in Harry's Bakery chapter*.

The Methodist Church at Surface Hill played an important part in both Rosalyn's and my lives. We spent our whole growing up years at Concerts, Preaching, 18 and 21st birthday parties, Engagement parties, Marriages, and Christenings.

Saturday night, 19th May 1945, the day before my 16th birthday, we were having a Christian Endeavour Convention Weekend. The church was alive, and I gave my life to my saviour Jesus Christ.

Rosalyn and I were married in the church on the 20th January 1951 and our two eldest children, Lynette and Ken, were baptized there.

The 100 years celebration of our Church in 1990 was a wonderful time.

In January 2001 for our 50th wedding anniversary, we had the privilege of celebrating the Reaffirmation of our Wedding Vows with our four children beside us at Surface Hill.

Wesley Methodist Hall. Built where our No2 tennis courts were until 1953. Photo 2018

A very sad day for me when this church was de-consecrated. The memories will always be close to my heart.

*I can remember Condies' bakers all dressed in white and their long white aprons sitting on a wooden bench outside the main bakery door, all smoking. That was when the old wooden Methodist Church sat on block 30 facing Reef Street with its high double stairs coming down from each side of the porch. I watched six men remove this old church and roll it on logs and skull drag it with two-steel cables attached to the building. Two men worked the winches, one man on the handle each side. When the old church reached its new position, backing onto Barter Street behind the new brick church and next to the parsonage, it was restumped with 2' (61cm) stumps, where it sat for 81 years.

This building was moved again in 2019 to the bottom side of the brick church. All the buildings are Heritage Listed*.

Original Methodist Church that faced Reef Street. Photo 1986

Jessie Condie was the shorthand and typing teacher with the Commercial Course at the Gympie State High School. Jessie spent her complete teaching life at this school. She taught pupils over three generations. Jessie was also the superintendent of the big Methodist Sunday School opposite her home from 1930 to 1945 and was a wonderful friend to all the Methodist folk till she passed away in 1968. Her home was sold for removal to make way for commercial buildings. Her sister Elizabeth passed away in 1942.

11 Mulcahy Street. Photo 2018

Charles and Emily built a modern Queenslander in 1922 on acreage in Mulcahy Terrace.

My parents, Alma and Eldor Stark, bought acreage at 4 Turners Lane, the land running down to Commissioner's Gully and adjoining Charles and Emily's property, in 1932. Turners Lane finished at our big gate leading into our cow paddock with a walking track and a little footbridge crossing Commissioner's Gully with a turnstile at one end to stop the cattle and horses from getting out. The street name was changed to Thomas Street (after Gympie's Mayor) in 1936.

You should see Thomas Street now in 2020! Bitumen road and cement guttering and houses as far as the eye can see.

*Photo number #48 was taken in 1937 as my two sisters, Joyce and Beth, and I were fishing for Mary Cod in Commissioner's Gully. It was a lovely running creek those days.

This photo was taken by Miss Fay Smith who was the housekeeper for the Condie family*.

Photo #48 Joyce Beth and John Stark.
Photo 1937

The Cross on photo number 49 shows where we sat. Our parents' home can be seen on photo 49 as №1. (The white home facing Thomas Street).

All the families within hearing distance of Condie's home will never forget the white cockatoo in the cage hanging outside the kitchen window. He sang all day, only problem, all he sang was ALLEN! ALLEN! ALLEN! He never shut up! Even when Allen came home at around 1-2pm. My younger brother, Leonard, who recently celebrated his 80th birthday asked me if I remembered Condie's bird? I wonder what happened to him? Those days there was a drop of 20' (6m) to the ground, I'm sure many people wished the cage would fall*.

Photo #49. #1Starks. #2Craigs. #3 Doyles. #4 Pilkington.
X marks where my sisters and I sat fishing. Photo 1983

*Allen and Leslie approached my dad and asked permission to cross our land, saving themselves a long walk to get to their

brother Thomas' bakehouse at 11 Stewart Terrace. They wore quite a path over the years, and I spoke to Les quite often as I milked our cow each morning around 6am. Les was the dough maker for his brother Tom and worked all night*.

The Condie's, Stream's, and Stark's homes and O'Hanlon's dairy farm were on the edge of Gympie, 8 minutes' walk to the CBD and Mary Street.

Charles and Emily's mode of travel up to the end of 2nd World War was in a beautiful four-wheel, rubber tyred trap, kept in lovely condition and pulled by 2 trotters. The last time I saw it was in 1944, parked under their home in Mulcahy Terrace.

Henry Condie lived in the unit in the original bake house in Reef Street until Harry Brother's bought the business in 1952, before moving back into the family home in Mulcahy Terrace with his brothers, Allen and Leslie.

*After retiring back to Gympie in 1983, I was the Justice of the Peace attending Cooinda Nursing Home residents and I was called in this day to do some work for one of the residents. Imagine my surprise to see Henry Condie waiting for me. We spoke very little of the past. He was the last living child of Charles and Emily. He passed away 10 months later.

I always thought Henry carried a chip on his shoulders as he was never happy; boy or man*.

In 1938, Condie's made a very bad investment; they were talked into putting a newly invented Electric Travelling Oven into the bakery. It took up so much room and it cost so much to run that Charles cut his losses and stopped using it after a short time.

This machine sat in place until the bakehouse doors closed permanently in 1972.

Instead, they expanded again with a new section built on the western end. Brickie Thompson had since retired, and his son Russell had taken over the company.

Electric Travelling Oven used by W & J Condie

W & J Condie's Bakery was the only bakery in Gympie that had three brick ovens.

In 1955 this is the oven that Doug Roy and I managed. Our story is included with Harry's.

W & J Condie only made white and brown bread and buns and produced approximately 2,000 loaves per day. Condie's also hold the record for the longest baking family in the district; 1878 to 1952, when they sold to Harry Brothers - Bakers of Duke Street, Gympie.

FOR ALL OVEN ESTIMATES AND REQUIREMENTS

RUSS THOMPSON

14 POPES ROAD, ---- GYMPIE

Urgent Messages ---- Phone Gympie 253

Our Firm has had 40 years' experience in Queensland in
Oven Building and Furnace Construction

DO ANYTHING IN OVEN WORK

NO DELAY

Adequate Stocks of Oven Fittings always on hand
Best of Materials and Workmanship

OUR SPECIAL FIRE BOX
Has already stood tests for 14 years without
Replacement

All work guaranteed and will go anywhere in Queensland

OUR REPUTATION IS OUR GUARANTEE

Chapter 8

Isaac Branch — Baker
5, 5a, 7 Caledonian Hill/Apollonian Vale
1889-1936

"Good to the Last Crumb"
Branch's Better Brown Bread,
built Bouncing Bonny Babies

These were the catch cries right from the very beginning of Branch's baking history when Isaac and Maria Branch started their bakery in 1889. They took the mining leases that were available at 5, 5a, & 7 Caledonian Hill. Council renamed this portion of the road to Apollonian Vale in 1890.

Isaac built his home on block #7, a very steep block with a gully running through. Isaac and Maria had 8 children. Boys were Ernest, Charlie, Jack, George, Reg, and Billy. The Girls were Sarah and Jessie.

Isacc & Maria's Home. Photo 2018

The Branch's knew they would need horses and carts to deliver their bread to customers and placed an order for two horse drawn delivery carts with the local Coach and Body Builder, Mr. Jack Smith of Monkland Street, better known to all of us as Jacky.

*Jacky's property came right out into the middle of the street. He had gear everywhere! His workshop was a dirt floor and sloped up the gradient of the hill.

I was with my father one day and Jacky was working out in the middle of the road as usual when he was nearly run over by a Whippet car.

People complained to the council and the inspector visited Jacky and told him to stay on his land behind the curb. Jacky saw red and practically dragged the man out into the middle of Monkland Street and had great delight in showing this gentleman the 2" (5cm) round surveyor's peg, right in the middle of the road.

It was the year 1972 before the council got its way. It was only when Jacky jnr. and his son took up land in the new industrial estate that it finally came to a head. Gympie was so mixed up with crooked roads. Just stand at the five-ways and look around. Streets like Mellor, Lawrence, Mary, and Calton Hill. Nearly all the streets in Gympie have bends in them as they followed around between the mines*.

1939 Coventry Eagle. Paid £25($50) second-hand.

I can remember when I took the petrol tank from my 1939 Coventry Eagle motorbike to Jacky. The dirt roads were so rough, the tap that was soldered into the petrol tank would break out and I would lose all my petrol.

Mary Street was tarred first. I remember the day they started Lawrence Street at the five-ways. This street ran up past our old Central Boys School.

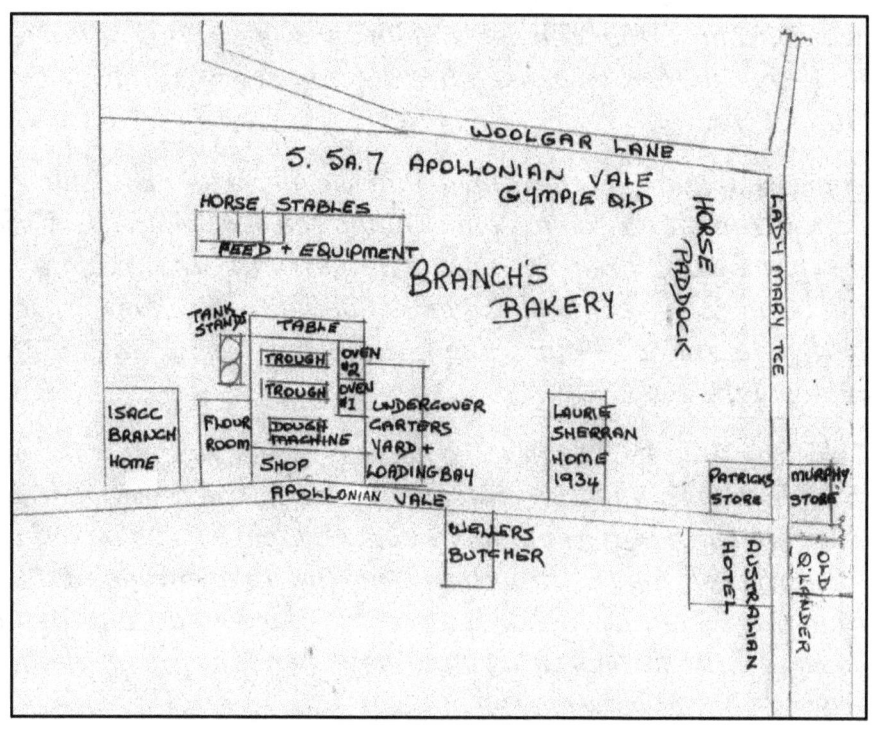

Mud map of Branch's property, Gympie

Branch's blocks went right through to Woolgar Lane, giving him plenty of horse paddocks.

He built, with the help of many family members, horse yards, stables, and associated buildings.

The N^{o.}1 oven was built with an internal fire and put to work immediately. While the delivery carts were being built, he canvassed the large populations still coming to Gympie to start his business.

"Branch's better brown bread built bouncing bonny babies"

Branch's Bakery
Caledonian Hill, Gympie

Left to Right: Wacky Flynn and "Old Tilly", Ted Stark and delivery truck, Eddie Branch and terraplane delivery van, Grandma Maria Branch (wife of Isaac Branch), Charlie Branch, Albert Prusse (apprentice, cousin of Noel J. Branch), Jack Branch (baker) Lloyd Window (apprentice, brother-in-law to Jack) Bill Branch and Splinter (1st bread cart), Reg Branch and ? (2nd bread cart)

Bread Prices: 2 Loaves at 2lb for 7 and a-half pence
1 Loaf at 2 lb for 4 pence

Appolian Vale Gympie
1930

You can see from the photo they all worked to enhance the business. Billy Branch was delivering out into the far area of Pine Street.

It was only a short while before Isaac was ordering another oven to be built by Bricky Thompson snr. It was at this time he had $^{No}1$ oven changed to a side firebox and the $^{No}2$ oven was bricked in and joined to $^{No}1$.

In 1902 Isaac heard about a dough mixing machine.

Up to this point all doughs were made by hand and Kerosene lights were still in use. The dough makers always started work between 7 & 8pm to start preparing the doughs for the following day. It's a wonder, now at the ripe old age of 92, that I can see at all*.

The dough mixing machine was ordered and the drum mixer finally arrived by steam train from Brisbane. People mistakenly said that Branches were putting in a steam boiler, because the mixing bowl was an 8' (2.5m) cylinder with a diameter of 3½' (1.06m). The framework was 7' (2m) off the floor. The installers had to take portion of the front wall out to get it inside.

I made doughs in this machine 47 years later.

The steel work was enormous! You had to climb 6 vertical steel stairs to a platform that ran the complete length and along one end of the mixer. The mixer had a door 4'x2' (1.5m x 0.6m) in the top side of the drum, and the door had 2 turn handles to secure it when the machine was working.

On the floor was a container to hold 1x 170lb (77kg) bag of flour. From this box a conveyor belt with cups attached carried the flour from the floor up to the door in the top of the mixer. Water had to be lifted manually by buckets and added to the flour along with Volmoyst (bread improver), salt, and liquid yeast.

In 1928, water was reticulated to the main area of Central Gympie from a reservoir at Watton Hill. In 2019 this now old, unused reservoir has been renovated into a beautiful home.

Branchs' also bought two motor vehicles. Both were turned into utilities with bread boxes for deliveries. Wacky Flynn drove one and called her "Old Tilly". The utility driven by Eddie Branch was originally a 1926 Terraplane car. When the Branchs sold the business, Eddie moved on with the family but Wacky kept on working there until James Fardoolie took over the bakery.

The dough recipe to make 300 loaves of bread used 3x170lb bags of flour and most ovens were built to cook 320 loaves. The recipe to make that amount of bread was the 3 bags of flour mentioned above plus 6 x 4-gallon (18.2 litre) buckets of water, 8lbs (3.6kg) of Volmoyst Bread Improver and 8lbs (3.6kg) of salt.

All doughs had to have a combined unit temperature of around 154°F (68°C) when the dough was finished.

You always started with the temperature of the flour. In Queensland you could adjust the dough temperature by adding hot or cold water (either from a tank, well, or bore) or by adding ice in later years. Before you shut the steel door and firmly secured it, you always checked to where your thermometer was, then you would climb down and start the steam, petrol, or crude oil engine or DC electricity from 1938.

Engage the bowl and the rumble would start. I pitied people attending the Baptist Church from 7.30pm two doors down. The dough machine would rumble for 20 minutes. You would stop mixing at 15 minutes, climb up, remove the door, and check how your dough was processing, altering the texture by adding flour or water as needed. Any sooner than that and you couldn't open the door. Then you would climb down and roll your first trough across the floor and place it in the exact position for the completed dough to fall into, remembering the height of the mixer door to the floor. When the mixing finished, you stopped the motor and locked the mixer in position so that the door stopped just below half way down, allowing the dough to slowly move forward. As the dough falls out of the mixer, you slice off large pieces and place them across the bottom of the trough. A sprinkle of flour and then cover the dough with empty flour bags allowing for the dough to rise.

In Gympie, all bakeries made eight, six, and four-hour doughs.

Originally all bakers started at 7am. On Monday morning the first bread delivery was not until about 8–8.30am while the carters waited for the first hot bread from the ovens. The rest of the week's first run was always of cold bread made the day before.

*In 1942, the Government allowed the bakers to start at 5am, then all deliveries were of hot bread coming straight from the oven at 6.45am. The carters started at 6am, giving them time to feed and harness their horses before loading their bread ready to leave the bakehouse at 7am.

Branch's dough machine was used for 55 years with never a breakdown. All that climbing up and down. The machine ended up at the scrap metal dealers at Monkland but should have ended its working life at the Gympie and District Historical Museum which was formed in 1970.

#5 Apollonian Vale replacing Branch's Bakery

*Billy Branch never left Gympie; he had the energy of 10 men; he ran everywhere. He spent his working life in bakeries. Firstly, working in his family's bakery then Sherrans, then Fardoolies. None of these bakeries made anything other than bread and buns.

Billy and his wife, May (nee Lowere), had 3 children, John, Gwen, and Keith and only lived a short distance away in Crown Road. Billy and May are buried in the Gympie Cemetery.

This section of Gympie was always busy. Motorised traffic coming into Gympie had to check their brakes before going down the steep hill to Mary Street. Horse drawn vehicles went via Lady Mary Terrace and Mellor Street into Mary Street.

Such a busy crossroad. A hotel on one corner, 2 small corner stores opposite each other and a lovely Queenslander on the other corner.

Lister/Wellers Butcher Shop was diagonally opposite the bakehouse.

Wedding of Billy Branch & May Lowere 1934

The Bruce Highway, when first named, went right through Monkland, Nashville, One Mile, Red Hill, Mary Street, Duke Street, and Pine Street down to the Two Mile and on to Maryborough.

*At Branchs, and in fact all bakeries, the dough makers were always busy through the night, making doughs for the orders and at 3am lighting the oven fires, knocking down the doughs in the troughs for the first time. When the doughs had rested for 20 minutes, it had its second knock down to make sure all the rising was removed and then was cut into big blocks and placed on the table, covered with a sprinkle of flour and empty flour bags. The bakers came in and had a cup of tea (which the dough maker had also made), they had a discussion with the foreman and the owners, making sure all was in hand and ready for them to start on the dot of 5am.

On days when the orders were smaller, the dough maker might lend a hand to the cutting up of the doughs before he headed for home, anytime from 7am or sometimes as late as 8.30am*.

I started my trade on a wage of 19/6d ($1.95), tradesmen earned £4 ($8) for a 48 hour plus week. Apprentices finished when the cleaning up was done, wood in, flour in, etc. No unions those days.

At that time, W & J Condie was the largest supplier to Gympie of bread and buns, with Branchs a close second and Longs coming in closely at 3rd.

The 4lb (1.8kg) tin loaves were the most popular. The farmers all asked for these as they said they kept better. This dough was first in right across the back of the oven, sometimes taking up half the space. This meant they were the last out. The 2lb (908g) loaves came out first and the 4 pounders were cooked to a further crispness. This gave the bread a finer texture and flavour.

My Dad was the first bread vendor in Queensland, working with Branch's Bakery. In the big photo taken in 1930, you can see him standing by his 1926 Rugby utility, wearing a "fair isle" vest, hat, and tie. My Mother always made sure he was well dressed. I included the full story in the Foreword. It wasn't long before I was accompanying him on his delivery rounds, I sat in the car and watched him until I started school. Then I always helped him on school holidays.

Government inspectors came twice a year to inspect your bakehouse, check your weights and measures. They always came in pairs. They would first check your scales against theirs, then stamp their inspector's number on the base. Then they checked all the weights, and they were also stamped.

*If your bakehouse had not been whitewashed over the past few years, smoke from the fires made quite a mess on walls and ceilings. The inspectors would tell you if the bakehouse had to be whitewashed from top to bottom. Every wall and ceiling glowed. Whitewash was all fire kilned lime to kill any germs.

Another job for a Thursday! Thursday was a light bread day as Carters had that day off because they had full deliveries on Saturday*.

Some years ago, my eldest son, Ken, and I were visiting a shopping centre on business and we stopped at a hot bread shop window and watched the baker prepare the dough. First cutting and weighing. He could see us watching and when I was writing on my notepad explaining the procedure to Ken, the baker must have mistakenly thought we were inspectors, because he went back over all his measured dough and added a piece to each one. We left after I explained to Ken why he had done that; he didn't have a clue who we were. We laughed and hoped he had learnt his lesson. All my baking days I was never charged for any underweight bread, although I have heard of a few bakers who were.

You only had to have the oven a little extra hot; that makes the dough steam a little more than it has to and bingo, you are in trouble. The inspectors were fair to us by weighing 8 loaves at a time to allow for variances. Your normal measure gave you about 104 to 107 two-pound loaves per 170lb bag of flour. I worked for one baker for a few months who required a little more water per dough and boy! trying to hand mould those loaves and only getting a few loaves extra made me wonder whether it was worth all the extra work that went into it. Doughs are very touchy. You really had to nurse your doughs to receive the best of finish, taste, and life.

All Gympie bakeries used wood from Brady's farms.

*I was over the moon one afternoon when talking to my daughter Lyn, the Branch name was mentioned.

My great grandson, Jai, was doing Saturday morning work with a Neil Branch in Gin Gin who just happened to be a descendant of Isaac Branch. Some weeks later Neil gave Ian and Lyn's son-in-law, Nicholas Brown, a photo of the Branch Bakery in Gympie with my dad standing proudly as the first Queensland bread Vendor in 1930. This gift is part of Gympie's history. My father also had this same photo, but it was lost over the decades*.

The phone rang one November morning 2019, and a voice stated: "I am Keith Branch, son of Billy Branch and I understand that you are in the process of writing the story of Gympie's Bakeries". Keith said that he would like to meet me and drove the 20 minutes from Buderim to Palmwoods and brought with him a framed 2'x18" photo of the 1930s Branch Bakery with all the staff and asked me to present it to the Gympie Library, courtesy of the Branch Family, which I did in January 2020.

I have spoken a few times to Keith since then and he said that he had received a letter from the Gympie Library thanking him for the donation*.

*Keith worked as an officer in the Queensland Fire Brigade stationed at Maroochydore and lives in Buderim.

I knew his father, Billy, from 1932–1953 and worked with him at Fardoolies Bakery for 10 months in 1949. He was my "jobber" on No.2 oven. A jobber was the name for the oven man's offsider*.

I thank cousins Keith and Neil Branch. Together we have been able to confirm old stories.

In 1936, Branchs told my dad they had put the bakery on the market. It was bought by Sherrans of Brisbane.

Sherrans also agreed to Dad's pricing structure that he had had in place with Branchs and so the delivery business continued. Sherrans had never heard of the 'vendor system' before this.

Jack and Charlie Branch moved to Maryborough and bought a bakery. Charlie and Agnes (nee Ogden) had 7 children, Edna, Noel, Robbie, Phyllis, Joan, Hazel, and Laurie.

Noel married Alexine Alpha Wilschefski and had 4 children, Noel Jnr, Neil, Sue, and Dennis. Noel did his trade with his father in Maryborough then moved to Mundubbera, Maleny, and Mt. Perry where he bought his first bakery. He sold that bakery and bought in Meandarra, then Mitchell, and finally settling in Gin Gin, where eventually his son, Neil, took over the business. Neil married Jenny and had 3 children, Anthony, Helen, and Angela. Neil and Jenny have 9 grandchildren. They now lease out the bakery.

Bread Roll & Bun Cutter - Courtesy of Neil Branch

Chapter 9

Neil Bradford— Baker
82 Red Hill Road Gympie
1901-1936

In 1901 a young baker arrived with his wife in Gympie. He had high hopes of making his mark on Gympie's history. We know very little of where he came from or what happened to his family in future years, but we do know that he was building in the middle of a wide hub of industry.

Neil built a one oven bakery with a home attached facing Red Hill Road, then converted one of the front rooms into a shop. He carried his bread through the house passageway from the bakehouse.

Bradford's Bakery was burnt to the ground in 1936

I remember going to Bradford's bakery in about 1934 with my dad. I do not remember any contact after then.

In the photo there has been nothing rebuilt at the old bakery site in 86 years.

82 Red Hill Road, Gympie. Photo 2018

In later years, friends of mine, Keith and Eunice Milliner, bought the property 43 Smyth Street directly behind No 82 Red Hill Rd and to their surprise found No 82 was attached to their deeds. Recently I have been advised that Keith & Eunice's son, Neil, has inherited the property. Maybe he might do something with this land*.

I presume that Bradford's trade would have been taken up by all the other bakeries.

What I do know is that my dad did not buy any bread from Neil Bradford.

*Shops and homes like Bradford's were built with that floor plan for many a small bakery; a refurbished version can be seen today (2022) in the little town of Beerburrum, closer to Brisbane.

This old bakehouse is now a beautifully restored private home. In 2019, the new owners invited me in and asked plenty of questions over cups of tea while we were sitting in the old kitchen.

Original Beerburrum Bakery

The owner has restored the home to its original condition. The bake house is fifteen feet behind the home and is falling down, only the roof and parts of the front and back wall along with the flour room still stands. He is hoping that in the future, he will *be able to restore it all. The oven was removed many years ago and the bricks were used for other buildings.*

It was a lovely afternoon remembering days of when I was employed by Norm Searle. I stood in my bedroom, which was at the front right of the building, across the hallway was the shop. The owner asked me to draw rough plans of the bakehouse, which I did for him, and he wanted to hear what it was like when I worked there. I showed them where the water bore used to be. Sadly, it was filled in by previous owners. The bore supplied all our water for the bakehouse. A huge Moreton Bay Fig tree grows right in the middle of the old driveway. Now there is a new entrance from the side street.

I spent 3 months baking there back in 1948 — no electricity, all handmade bread, and cakes. I was waiting for a position to become available at Fardoolies in Gympie. Harrys had nothing available for me at that time.

I was keeping company with Rosalyn Pritchard (my future wife). Each weekend I used to ride my 1946 Royal Enfield along the dirt road to Gympie to see her*.

Chapter 10

Reg Sherran and Sons -Bakers
5, 5a, 7, Apollonian Vale Gympie
1934-1948

The year 1934 had just begun. The word had moved around the bakery world that Gympie was very prosperous.

At a bakehouse in Oxley Drive, Sherwood, Brisbane, Reg's sons, Ross and Laurie, were very restless. With the depression, their trade in Brisbane had reached its peak. They asked their father to put the bakehouse on the market to sell the lease and it sold overnight to a new baker in the Brisbane area, Mr Bernie McKenna.

I worked relieving Bernie when he owned his Stanthorpe bakery. Rosalyn and I were doing relieving work for The Bread Manufacturers of Queensland, Brisbane, when our eldest daughter, Lynette, was only 8 months old.

Within a month, Sherrans had bought Branch's Bakery and could not believe the size and height of Branch's dough making machine.

They too had never seen a vendor who bought bread at wholesale prices and being in competition with the baker's own horse and cart & utility deliveries. Dad and the Sherrans worked out a wholesale price, with a special price to retail shops like Mrs MacDonald over on the South Side. The senior Sherran family moved into the main house at No7. Ross had married and built a new home on No5.

*One thing I will always remember, as a boy of eight I delivered two hot loaves of fresh bread to the wife of the Chief of the Fire Station. I put them on her table and left.

My Father was not very happy with me. The two hot loaves took the French polish off her table. I supposed that my father would have paid to have the table repolished. I was told that it left two long imprints*.

When my father and his two mates were recalled by letter into the P.M.G. Department in 1937. Dad showed Mr Sherran the letter and he agreed to buy the two runs off Dad.

#5 Apollonian Vale - Ross Sheeran's home

Billy Branch didn't want to shift his family as the children were settled in Gympie schools, so he decided to stay on and work with the Sherrans. Billy Branch delivered in his horse and cart, right out to Iron Street. Rosalyn's parents had Branch's and Sherran's bread delivered up till 1939. Sherrans employed Norm Ganley to take over dad's deliveries with a 2nd horse and cart.

World War II was declared in September 1939 and the Government Department of Defence (D^D) was formed. They were now in control of all the fuel and food production in Australia. The owners of the five bakeries in Gympie, Mr Charles Condie from W & J. Condie, Mr. Bill Blakeway, Mr. Fred Weller, Mr Reg Sherran, and Mr Tom Condie all received a letter marked with the official stamp of OHMS (On His Majesty's Service) on the envelope and telling them to be at the Soldiers Hall in Reef Street at 10 am, on the 10th of December and no explanation why! Not knowing the reason for this meeting caused quite a discussion between the bakers.

The D^D brought with them Mr Jack Jamerson, the Returned Service League's Gympie Secretary, to chair the meeting.

On the 10th of December, the D^D men arrived, and they explained that the huge area of Gympie now covered by the five bakeries, was to be divided into five delivery areas. They told the bakers, who were in surprise, that they would save on fuel, distribution costs, and on wear and tear of vehicles and animals.

Today's generation say big brother is watching! Well! way back in 1939, he sure was! We already had received identity cards the size of a C5 envelope to produce when asked.

These Government gentlemen knew more about Gympie than you thought they should have! Then they laid out on the big table in the alcove of the Soldiers Hall plans of their division of the Gympie bread runs. They called for a break in the proceedings for about an hour. Shock was the word that was used by the bakers. The government had numbers, places, details — even down to the two shops in Mary Street of Bill Blakeway and Tom Condie. The bakers had no say. The D^D had all the answers. The bakers were given their new areas and had to start work in them in six weeks, which fortunately gave them some time to organise their new runs.

The owners of the bakeries had no come back and yes, they had some mix ups for a few weeks. I know at one intersection of three runs the baker's carts were seen to meet up. But after twelve months, they all agreed that they had saved money, wear and tear on equipment and animals and that they would carry on. They really never went back to their old ways of doing business after the war.

W & J Condie were in the centre of town, so held onto the contract to supply all the Hospitals Refreshment Rooms and Hotels etc. Supplying the refreshment rooms was a very lucrative order, requiring the three ovens.

*The Refreshment Rooms in Gympie supplied all the troops, coming and going, with a meal and a couple of slices of bread and butter. The butter was supplied locally in 56lb (25.4kg) boxes by the Gympie Co-op Butter Factory (Golden Nugget). The Refreshment Room ladies had one of the large electric

Bacon cutters, it was run by the city electric light company, now in operation with Direct Current (DC).

Block of land where the Railway Refreshment Rooms Single Ladies Quarters 1936 -1952. Replaced by the Gympie's Railways Institute.

All the ladies took turns in cutting the four-pound square sandwich white bread loaves. The single ladies who worked in the Refreshment Rooms were boarded in quarters near the overhead walkway to Lady Mary Terrace*.

Railway Refreshment Rooms - Single Ladies Quarters. 1881 - 1926

I always liked going to the bakehouse with my dad, I scored a bun if any were around. Dad always picked up his two-pound white rolls which could be broken and sold in halves. In 2020, they call them "high top loaves".

The four-pound white was known as a 'tin loaf'. The two-pound white was a 'full loaf.' A half loaf was known as a 'quarter'. Queensland and Victoria were the only States that called their bread by these terms.

After the war started, the scarcity of work immediately disappeared. Our men and women went into the Air Force, Army, and Navy. The girls joined the Land Army, except for those who were on essential services.

Reg Sherran employed Norm Ganley on the second horse and cart. He and Billie Branch stayed at Fardoolie's until all the local bakeries were out priced by Tip Top Bakeries. They bought out all the small bakeries throughout Brisbane, Ipswich, and Sunshine and Gold Coast areas, closed them down, and used some of the buildings as depot's in lieu of the onslaught of supermarkets and hot bread shops*.

*Dough machines were now a standard U shape at floor level. I put one into my bakery at Amamoor.

I am sure Mrs Sherran next door took some months trying to get to sleep at night, with that terrible rumble*.

Bread prices in England had stood still for 50 years. In Sydney the price started as one and a half penny for a two-pound loaf. Farthings ceased to be legal tender in Australia in 1914, but somehow the bread prices, had stayed in farthings till the 1970s*.

*Strange, I do not know what names they use for bread today. What they call a brown loaf or what they call the size of bread. I personally do not like brown or wheatmeal — never have.

Brown bread has always been in a square bottom tin, I still have one in my collection today.

I do not know what Dad did with his leftover bread each day. You could never exactly know what your customers' needs would be. When I had my own bakehouses, very rarely, if ever, did I sell out before the end of the day.

The Sherrans sold the bakehouse to James Fardoolie in 1948. They then returned to their bakery at Sherwood, Brisbane.

Bernie McKenna had bought a bakery at Stanthorpe. I relieved Bernie for a month in 1952 when I was working through the Breadmaker's Association.

IMPORTANT

Re BREAD PRICE.

Dear Sir,

Approval has been given for an increase of a farthing in the price of all delivered bread to take effect from Monday next, the 5th November 1951. This increase is on delivered bread only and is applicable to Standard, Starch Reduced and Sliced and Wrapped Bread.

The price of bread in your town is as follows:

STANDARD BREAD | Wholesale | Bakehouse & Shop | Delivered
| 9¾ | 10½ | 11 |

STARCH REDUCED BREAD

An Official announcement will be made through the Press on Saturday, 3rd November 1951.

With compliments.

Yours sincerely,

D.C. Black,
Secretary.

DCB:JS.

P.S. An additional ½d. has been granted for your town following on the recent adjustment on Rail Freights.

Letter arrived telling us what and when our bread prices would increase.

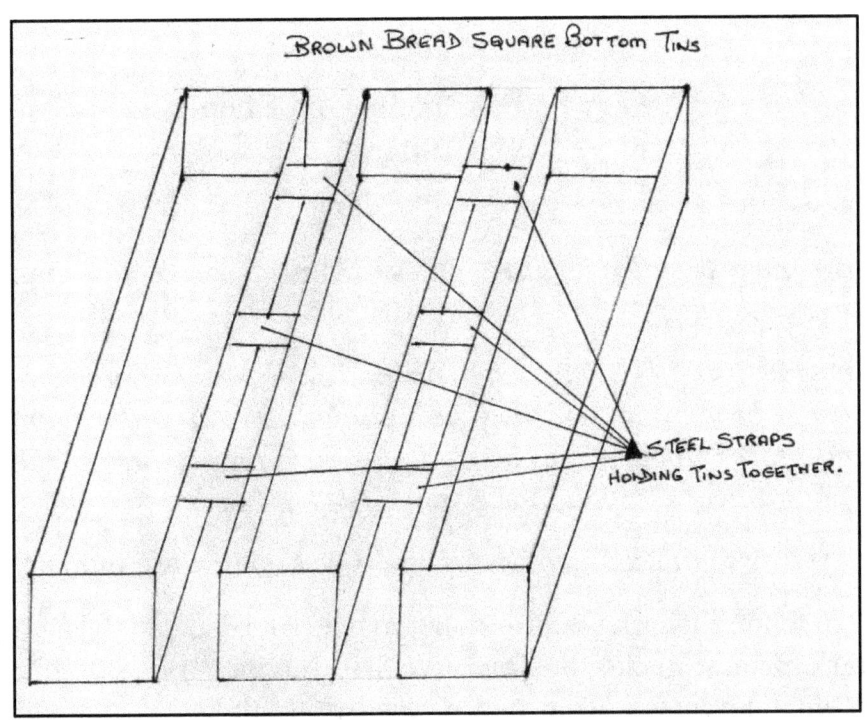

Brown Bread Square Bottom Tins

Chapter 11

Thomas Condie
137 Mary St Bakehouse and Shop
1929-1934

Thomas, son of Charles, grandson of James.

Tom as he was called by all, expressed himself to me "as a man not to tangle with".

He showed his true colours when my dad approached him to buy wholesale bread and also how he handled the Australian and United States troops when he sold pies from his pie cart at the Gympie Railway Station in the years 1941-1943.

As a young man I found only Allen & Les Condie ever smiled.

In 1929 when the great depression started, Tom decided to leave his father's and uncle's business (W & J Condie — Bakers) and start out for himself. Tom had noticed that Blakeway's Bread Shop in Mary Street was doing very well. Tom approached John Balthes, the Jeweller who owned several blocks around Mary Street, and an agreement was made allowing Tom to build a small bakehouse in the laneway behind one of John's shops, even though his opposition was diagonally opposite in Mary Street. Tom thought he would try and take some of the bread trade away from Blakeways'.

In Mary Street there were large firms employing many staff. Bill Blakeway was supplying them with "hot" sausage rolls (Bill had the first electric warmer in Gympie), along with buns and coffee rolls. Bill also ventured into Block and Christmas Cakes. His brother Stanley took control of the Cake Making Section. Bill had also bought the first cake mixer powered by electricity.

Laneway to Condies bakehouse

Tom Condie had Brickie Thompson and his son Russell build his new internally fired oven holding 120 loaves and when finished sold his goods from the bakehouse door. Six months later business was going so well that he rented a small shop from John Balthes fronting Mary Street.

the past year was £389, which was a little over £100 in excess of the profit from the previous year, the cost of producing the Journal is rapidly mounting, due mainly to the difficulty of obtaining suitable paper and the fact that pap ercosts are rising rapidly. I have endeavoured to offset this increased cost by the writing of additional advertisements and other economies with regard to blocks, etc., but it appears likely that some increase in advertising rates will have to be made in the next 12 months if the standard of the Journal is to be maintained.

In conclusion I would make the point that the work of an Association such as ours is a continuing one. Many problems such as price, labour, deliveries and so on need constant and unremitting attention. It is when conditions are unstable that a Trade Association does most good. In thanking the President, Executive, Council Members and the small but loyal and efficient staff for their unstinted co-operation over the past year, I look forward to their continued support in the coming year, which promises to be as difficult as the period just completed.

D. C. BLACK,
Secretary.

Annual Meeting

T. B. CONDIE RE-ELECTED PRESIDENT

The Annual Meeting of the Association held on the 13th June, 1951, saw the greatest attendance to an Annual Meeting for many many years. No less than 40 members were present at the meeting, including a number of bakers from the Lockyer centre. This meeting showed clearly the greater interest that is now being shown in Association affairs by rank and file members and augurs well for the Association's work in the coming 12 months.

The main business of the meeting was the election of officers, and the returning officer, Mr. D. C. Black, announcing the result of the ballot, declared that Mr. T. B. Condie had polled 96 votes and Mr. D. B. Nunn 53 votes, so that Mr. Condie was thus elected State President for the Association for the ensuing 12 months. For the position of City and Country Vice-Presidents, the only nominations received were from Mr. Jack Sheeran and Mr. Paul Sander respectively, and so they were elected to these positions unopposd. Similarly with the office of Treasurer, which was filled by Mr. George

Highly Successful Council Meeting

- Increased Profit Margin.
- Report on "Convenient Point" deilvery.
- Paper Supplies Difficult.
- Variations to Northern Awards.
- Review on Flour Tonnages.
- Delegates appointed for Federal Executive meeting.

The Council of Management Meeting held in Brisbane on the 12th and 13th June once again showed only too clearly the advantages that accrue when Country Delegates representing the rank and file members have an opportunity of discussing matters of importance to the trade. It is in this way that members far removed from Brisbane are able, through their delegate, to exercise a voice in the control and policy of the Association.

Delegates came to Brisbane from as far North as Cairns and Officers of the Association were enabled to gauge the feeling of Country members on many important items which came up for discussion.

The meeting commenced before lunch on Tuesday and was chaired by the Association President, Mr. T. B. Condie. Other Delegates were Mr. G. A. Holmes, Vice-President; Mr. D. B. Nunn, Immediate Past-President; Mr. L. W. Enever and Mr. A. A. Dance, Brisbane Branch; Mr. P. Sander, Ipswich; Mr. G. B. Mills, Far North; Mr. A. W. Bobin, South Burnett; Mr. G. Hamilton, Mackay; Mr. K. J. Todd, Rockhampton; Mr. B. McKenna, Stanthorpe; Mr. S. Axelsen, Maryborough; Mr. F. Frehner (Pastrycook Section), and Mr. D. C. Black, Secretary.

Apologies were received from Mr. Boy Turner, of Townsville, who, due to unforeseen circumstances, was unable to attend, and from Mr. N. R. Anderson, of Toowoomba.

After the Minutes of the previous meeting held in Gympie on the 6th and 7th March, 1951, had been read and confirmed, the Auditor's Report, Income and Expenditure Account and Balance Sheet were received and some discussion took place concerning the financial standing of the Association.

Delegates present expressed gratification at the fact that notwithstanding the unforeseen and additional expenditure, in the

*The Thompsons were very close friends of my Father and Mother. Their children Ruth, Russell, and Marjorie were born around the same time as us. We all went to Sunday School

together. Ruth and Russell both married and moved to Canberra. Unfortunately, they didn't have any children and that line of the Thompson family died out in March 2002 with the death of Marjorie*.

Tom only produced bread and buns at the bakehouse. When his lease with John Balthes was up, the contract stated he had to demolish the bakery and leave clear ground.

He'd had steady trade over the past 4 years, but used to say, "nothing to write home to mother about". When he opened his new Bakery in Stewart Terrace in 1934, Tom was a man of few words and at this time, was still living at home with his parents.

In 2020, where Tom's bakery was situated is now a bitumen car park.

Clear ground where Condie's laneway bakehouse stood.

Chapter 12

Fred Weller, Baker
261—263 Brisbane Road Monkland Gympie
1922-1965

The year was 1922 and no new bakers had ventured into the Monkland area for 13 years. This young man, a distant cousin to William Thomas Weller's family, came to Gympie and purchased two mining leases on Brisbane Rd. The heavy deep mining of the area had just about petered out.

Where Fred Weller's bakehouse and home stood.

Runges and Archibalds were deep mining in Cracow during the Gold Rush of 1896. They came back to Gympie to look into re-opening "in tribute" "The Scottish Gold Mine" on Brisbane Road covering a huge 46 acres of land, which they did from 1933 to 1948.

Fred, like others before him, required the expertise of Bricky Thompson to build an oven for him to take around 300 loaves. Mr Thompson told Fred that he would need two ovens and proposed to build two ovens at a reduced price, which Fred accepted. Mr Glover and Mr Stream built the bakehouse, and on the adjoining property they also built a two-bedroom miners' cottage.

Fred employed two carters driving utilities with bread boxes on the back. He canvassed the area. What made Fred's business a success was the five-way split by the D^D in 1939.

He delivered bread to Pa and Mrs Runge, Billy & Beth Runge, Irv & Joyce Runge (my sister), and John & Marcy Runge and families. He delivered bread from 1932 to the bakehouse closure in the 1960's. Fresh bread Monday to Saturday except for Thursday (the carter's day off). Fred's Bakehouse only produced bread and buns.

John Stark with Wal Bentley. 2021

Over the years I have known Fred's staff. Wal Bentley started his trade in 1948 and spent 13 years working at this bakehouse. Fred's son, Ron Weller, joined his dad and completed his trade. Names like Les McGinnis, (I worked with Les for Harry Brothers in Reef Street). Darcy Bradford was Fred's Foreman (a son of Neil Bradford, who had his bakehouse burnt down in 1936). Jack Evers was his dough maker. Over the years Lester McKewen, Jack Smith, Les Meads, Ron Stokes, Alan Weller, and Stan Betts all worked for Fred Weller and others in Gympie and District.

Fred did not keep up the new machines. Wal told me he had a Cummings Dough Machine with a splash guard that acted as a clutch, you lifted the guard which in turn disconnected the belt driven from a 12hp petrol engine. All the doughs were manhandled from the troughs to the ovens.

Fred just closed his doors in 1965.

It was sad to see the trade slipping away, the hype of sliced bread in the supermarkets came into being. First the bread came from the large conglomerate bakeries in Brisbane, brought through by big cam decks delivering to depots in each town on their way north. In Gympie, Woolworths put into place their own bakery. Coles in the main street allowed Bakers Delight into their store. Then a couple of Hot Bread shops and the rest is history.

February 2020 was the first time in 61 years that I had been in a bakery. Everything is stainless steel; you could see your face everywhere. Now, a travelling oven (like a rotisserie) produces all varieties of bread. With electric weighing machines you do not need to be a baker anymore, only a machine operator.

Chapter 13

Bill Blakeway - Baker
72-74 Duke Street Gympie.
1935-1944

Bill Blakeway, working at the Spring Hill Bakery wanting to make a better life for his wife and daughter, found out by word of mouth from a baker in Brisbane that Henry Long in Gympie was wanting to retire.

Bill phoned Henry and arranged to catch the train to Gympie and then took Mr Bickle's taxicab to Duke Street where he found Henry in the breeze way stirring the potatoes in the fire place, making the yeast for that night's doughs.

Mud map of Bill Blakeways home, breezeway and bakehouse.

Henry Long, now well into his seventies, had been the baker at this end of Gympie for 53 years and was looking to retire. Bill and Henry, when they met, clicked straight away and two weeks later when Bill brought his wife, Dorothy, and daughter, Shirley, to Gympie, they settled the sale. When Bill got back to Brisbane, he went to visit his brother Stan working at Nundah Bakery and told his brother what he had bought and offered him the position of ovens man on the $^{No}2$ oven, which he accepted.

Bill and Dorothy now had three weeks to pack all their belongings and have them on a goods train to Gympie. Their belongings were then delivered by one of the six carriers to their new home next door to the bakery.

Stan & Flo Blakeway's home. 2021

Stan and his wife, Florence, rented a home from Mrs Cox, just round the corner in Jane Street and they shifted their belongings the same way as Bill and Dorothy. Stan had to give two weeks' notice at Nundah and only had a week to completely shift and be ready to start work in Gympie.

In later years when I started my apprenticeship, Stan and Florence literally took me under their wing, especially when I courted and married Rosalyn. We stayed close friends till they passed away in Bundaberg in the 1980s.

Bill had many apprentices over the years. The men I remember were Ray Redlinker, David Byrnes, and Ivan Smith.

I am afraid time has caught up with me on the names of the boys from so far back. I am sure Ted and Abe would have mentioned them, although the staff never changed much over all those years.

Steve Heilbronn, of 9 Pine Street, worked with horse and cart until Bill bought a new Morris in 1938 and had it converted to a panel van for Steve to deliver the small city run every day and the Calico/McIntosh Creek run three days a week. Henry Heilbronn, a nephew of Steve, was the other carter for Bill and started as a lad of 16.

The men working for Henry Long stayed with Bill Blakeway and Stan took over as baker on oven #2 with Bill working where he was needed.

Steve spent the rest of his working life with Blakeways, Reg Harry, Harry Brothers, and Cliff Harry incorporating W & J Condie, and retired in 1952.

Those days most married men never changed their jobs. Once settled into work you stayed put. Some were like me and went on to buy our own Bakeries after the Second World War.

Bills' greatest move was to find a shop in town and sign a good lease. Dorothy employed the shop staff, and all went well. Bill also bought a second-hand Bedford Panel Van to do the deliveries to the shop. All the deliveries of bread, trays of buns, cakes, etc. were delivered to the back entrance of the shop in Reef Street. The door was up six steep stairs which had to be negotiated carrying each tray.

In 1940 Bill traded in his one arm dough machine for a new Sterling Dough Machine & Rim extension. He also bought a Sterling Moulder & Cutter and a new Peerless Cake Mixer.

MORE AUSTRALIAN BAKERS

Use

The machine with the patented uncopyable "Floating Roller" that does not fell the dough.

MOULDERS
THAN ALL OTHER MAKES PUT TOGETHER!

SINCE BAKERS ALWAYS "TALK AMONGST THEMSELVES"—THERE CAN BE ONLY ONE REASON FOR THIS STRIKING FACT—

"STERLING" MOULDERS MUST BE GIVING BAKERS EVERYWHERE COMPLETE SATISFACTION

Sterling Service built "Sterling" Success;
Service during the Depression.
Service in the Pre-War Years;
Service throughout the War;
Service in the present Reconstruction Period;

Service Guaranteed in the Future by "STERLING'S" ESTABLISHED STABILITY

- They MUST be properly designed, constantly improved, soundly engineered— and the RIGHT PRICE.
- They MUST be doing a thoroughly efficient job, saving Time, Money and Labour, and turning out Good Bread under all conditions, in bakeries LARGE, MEDIUM and SMALL.
- They MUST be backed by real Service in the past (18 years of it!), and service assured in the future by a solidly-established here-to-stay firm.

(Protected by Patents)
PROMPT DELIVERY FOR ORDERS PLACED NOW

OTHER "STERLING" BAKEHOUSE UNITS
Dough Mixers
Tempering and Measuring Tanks
Aerator-Sifters
Dividers
Rounders
Automatic Proovers

STERLING MACHINERY PTY. LTD.
Head Office and Works:
596-598 Prince's Highway, St. Peters, Sydney.
Telephones: LA1516 and LA1257
Telegrams: "Mixers, Sydney"

Queensland Agent:
C. H. WATSON & CO.
65 Albert Street, Brisbane
Telephones: B3355 and B3356

DUKE and MARY STREET

PHONE 42   GYMPIE,..19......

Mr. & Mrs..

Dr. to Wm. A. Blakeway
BAKER and PASTRYCOOK
ACCOUNTS STRICTLY WEEKLY

							£	s.	d.
To Account Rendered									
Mon.	Tues.	Wed.	Thurs.	Fri.	Sat.	Total			
		Total							

C. & S. LOAVES....................................

BUNS & TEA CAKES..............................

MALT LOAVES......................................

CREDIT BY CASH..................................

BALANCE..

£..................

Bill Blakeway's Customers Monthly Account Docket

He had great hopes for the future. *The bakers had a lot of sitting around waiting time. I don't remember any baker who did not smoke, except me, "a come along Church Boy".

My father was a chain smoker until the day that it was announced that we were at war. He finished his last block of tobacco and stated, "No More" and he kept his word, he never lit another cigarette.

I tried a pipe and burnt my tongue. The pipe still lies in my draw. Never broke it in.

I used to go skiing each year, staying at Perisher Valley Lodge in the New South Wales snow fields. I thought the pipe would go well with all who sat around the big log fire in the bottom lounge. One year they bought me home strapped up in elastic bandages. Rosalyn never let me go again, my ski gear is still in the wardrobe.*

Many stories are told as to what happened in the old days when everything was handmade. Doughs were a massive job. Two and a half hours to make the dough for 300 loaves with sweat and tobacco ash falling into the mixture. Summertime was terrible on the dough maker in a hot bakehouse. I used to use rag head bands and have sweat rags tucked in my belt to wipe away any fluid. Very hard on your shoulders. In my later years, my shoulder tendons snapped and both shoulders had to be operated on. I have metal in my right arm from my neck to my elbow. Today all I can lift is 20 kilos (if I'm lucky). I do not have any strength.*

Bill Blakeway must have completed a course on Pastry Cooking, because he ventured into pastry in a big way.*

Bread forms were changing. By 1940 a good half of your oven load was round bottomed 2lb normal top loaf (Normal top is now known as high top). Brown always stayed the square bottom loaves, able to be broken in half in the middle, or as one rolled long loaf. All bread tins were greased with butchers dripping, *giving that beautiful flavour and aroma. On a cold winter's morning, when the oven man opened the damper to allow the steam out before he opens the door, this gorgeous smell floated all over, telling the townspeople the bread is coming out and the customers who lived close by started arriving*.*

Former home of Bill & Dorothy Blakeway in Monkland St.

After selling the business to Reg Harry in 1944, Bill retired and bought a home in Monkland Street.

*I remember when Col McBride and I took Shirley Blakeway to the pictures one Saturday night. I was sure green, I paid for Shirley's ticket and Col took her home. I never came into that game again. Once bitten twice shy

Not long afterwards they sold their home to Mr. & Mrs Wood. Their daughter Joyce married Ted Harry in 1946.

I believe the Blakeways moved to Buderim. Some years later, talking to Stan and Florence I heard that Shirley was married and living in Brisbane. That was over 60 years ago*.

Chapter 14

Thomas Condie—Baker and Pastry Cook
11 Stewart Terrace Gympie
1932-1956

Tom could not cover what he had planned for his business at his little bakehouse in the lane off Mary Street.

He bought a property at 11 Stewart Terrace, between Gibsons Brothers – Butchers, and Peter Dautel - Grocer of Distinction.

11 Stewart Terrace

The three shops go well together, Butcher, Baker, and Grocer. My Mum and Dad were account customers of Dautels. They spread their monthly buying over three firms. Dautels, 13 Stewart Terrace. Nosworthys, 7 Mary Street, and Thurecht's, 202 Mary Street.

Tom also bought the land at 19 Stewart Terrace on which, a few years later, he built a new brick home. Tom was the only one of the Condie boys to marry and he wed late in life; they had no children.

Thomas again approached Bricky Thompson and his son Russell to build the new ovens. By this time, modern improvements had been introduced. Both ovens were equipped with thermometers, electric lights and were oil fired instead of wood. The firebox was still in the bottom right-hand corner of the oven but now had an oil pipe plumbed into it. A lot easier for the oven man and apprentices.

Each oven held approximately 300 loaves.

Tom kept the Mary Street shop open using the side entrance in the lane for deliveries.

Tom Condie's former Mary St Bakery Shop

From Jacky Smith, Tom bought the latest in horse drawn delivery carts, with rubber tyred car wheels. The driver stood on the rear platform to control the horse.

Tom also bought a Hudson cab and chassis and had Jacky Smith build a complete panel van on the chassis. This van had a large back door to allow full trays to be loaded. Tom employed Mr Gibson of Louisa Street to be his main delivery man. A twin brother to the butcher next door to the bakehouse.

*I can still see this van parked in the lane off Mary Street, with Mr Gibson carrying trays into Tom's shop.

Mr Gibson always took the cream-coloured van home. He kept it spotless, always washed, and polished before he started work at 7am.

On Thursdays (carter's day off), Mr. Gibson would deliver fresh bread and cakes to Tom's town shop. Then Mr. Gibson would reload the panel van with cakes and deliver them to town run customers*.

Mr Gibson had twin boys, David & Laurie. David married Bricky Thompson's youngest daughter Marjorie. We all grew up friends*.

Tom's brother, Lesley, was his dough maker. Tom's other brother, Allen, left his father and uncle at W & J Condie of Reef Street to be Foreman for Tom. That only left Henry to work for their father and uncle.

Tom also employed Ossie Bowham as his Pastrycook.

I must admit Ossie was one of the best. I feel sure we admired each other's work displayed in the shops in Mary Street.

Tom's bakehouse staff were Viv Kaylor, Lindsay White, and Merv Webster. Colin Priddie was his carter who handled the horse and cart. Mr. Gibson was Tom's main carter.

Tom had a stationary pie cart built and placed it on the bank just outside the fence of the Gympie Railway Station.

*In 1943, his pie cart was completely destroyed. Lots of pieces scattered around the area and lots of different stories drifted around Gympie about the destruction.

All that is standing now are the last bits of the railway weighing machine. Tom personally staffed this pie cart, supplying pies and watermelons (in summer) to the Aussie and Yank troop trains*.

*In July 1951 Tom was re-elected President of the Bread Makers Association of Queensland. He excelled in leading the Association, obtaining Registration of bakeries and wage rises for the trade manufacturing of bread.

Tom Condie's Pie Cart was situated in between the 2 flags.

---

70   NEWS FOR THE BREAD MANUFACTURER OF Q'LAND   July, 1951

known to you all, and I, on your behalf, have wished them all the best in their future life.

I wish to extend my appreciation to the officials and executive of the Association for the wholehearted co-operation given me during my term of office. It was only the result of team work that so much has been achieved. To the Millers and Allied Traders I also extend my sincere thanks for their helpful advice and assistance.

I wish to pay tribute to the efficiency of the office staff and express appreciation for the assistance rendered to me and all manufacturers. Even though three major staff changes were made during the year—75 per cent. of the staff—efficiency did not suffer.

The Association to-day is able to and ready to cope with all work and meet all emergencies. Yes, indeed, we have been most fortunate with our choice of office staff.

I give this to you for consideration. The inflationary tendency throughout the whole of the community's economic life has made things very difficult for the baking industry, and were it not for the success that the Association has achieved in the prices field, it is very doubtful whether the industry would have survived.

It is certain that the next 12 months will be as difficult as the past ones have been, with regard to ever-increasing costs, and your Association officials must necessarily carry on unceasing negotiations with prices authorities so as to maintain bread prices at a reasonable level. If your Association is assured of your co-operation and support, well the fight is almost won.

T. B. CONDIE, President.

The world was told that **bread is the staff of life,** *and it must be always kept to the lowest price possible, so that all people,* *however poor, could always find enough coin to buy a loaf. I was told this on many occasions*.*

Tom would enter 4 x 4-pound Tin loaves each August in the Queensland National Show in Brisbane. For the show bread he made a special white dough. The dough had a special silky texture that was only achievable by making the dough by hand. Tom was very jealous of the recipe.

In 1952 he won Grand Champion and of course he would have all his cups and ribbons on display in the shop and on all his advertising*.

*I personally marvelled where Tom found the time to be involved in so many things.

When I left Gympie and couldn't supply my parents with my own bread, mother had Tom's horse and cart carter supply her bread until my father's transfer to Brisbane. He was promoted to Engineer in Charge of all the underground cables*.

In 1965, Tom was feeling that trade was slowly slipping so he sold out to Mr Cliff Harry.

In the late 1960's, Tom bought the old Blue Bird Café site and the land from Mary to Nash Streets. This café was opposite the Memorial Gates, where Tom built Condie's Arcade, which still stands today in 2022.

Tom Condie passed away 20.07.1989 and is buried in Gympie Two Mile Cemetery.

He was a hard-hitting businessman.

Chapter 15

Reg Harry—Baker and Pastry Cook
72—74 Duke Street Gympie
1944-1945

Mr. Reg Harry and his wife Kathleen had the bakery at Clermont in Central Queensland. They had two daughters, Beryl 16yrs and Eileen 12yrs.

Reg also had three sons from a previous marriage. His first wife had passed many years before. Cliff was the youngest at 18 years and had just finished his trade as a baker-pastry cook apprenticed to his father. Robert was 22 years, and Edward (known as Ted), 25 years. Ted already had a bakery at Home Hill, where with staff, he produced a wide variety of bread and cakes. Robert was not interested in being a baker and went into underground mining at Mount Isa in Western Queensland.

*The D^D hierarchy clamped down very heavily on those who tried to join their mates. Two of my mates — Cliff and Doug tried. Cliff left his father's bakehouse in Central Queensland, caught a train to Brisbane and enlisted. Four months into his basic training, the military police arrived at Redbank Training Camp and arrested him. The Army put Cliff,

Cliff Harry in Army uniform

accompanied by a sergeant, on a train and delivered him back to his father in Clermont.

Doug, the other apprentice, drifted into the drafting office in Brisbane, stated he was a baker (not an apprentice). Doug served in Dutch New Guinea. There were 140 men in Doug's unit, and he told me that when they were at last relieved and taken to Port Moresby the whole unit suffered badly from Dysentery after gouging themselves on T-bone steaks.

After the war had finished, it took Doug twelve months to regain his health and then another two years to finish his trade back with Harry's. We stayed friends and worked together at odd times throughout our early years in the bakeries. His full story is in Harry's chapter*.

Reg wanted to move his family closer to Brisbane, to be nearer to Kathleen's mother, Mrs Rooney, who lived at Toowong.

Before Christmas 1943 Reg discussed the matter of selling the businesses with Ted in 1944 and both families moving South. They placed both bakehouses on the market and both were sold within two weeks of each other. The call then went out through the baking world to find a business for sale large enough to accommodate these families. Sales reps of the Flour Mills were handy to any news of bakeries for sale or were thinking of selling. The rep from Seafoam Flour had heard that Bill Blakeway may be ready to relinquish his bakery in Gympie. Reg phoned Bill *(by that time telephones were becoming a little more common*).

My father was the Engineer for P.M.G.in Gympie. Our home telephone number was 465. Quite a few families used Joyce and I as 'message boys'. We objected as some families were just too far away. So, Dad put a stop to them using us for trivial messages, emergencies only. Our phone was at the end of the line in Thomas Street.

The sale went through and in four weeks another new baker and family were welcomed to Gympie and to the Surface Hill Methodist Church.

The Harry family were all beautiful singers. Kathleen was a Salvation Army Captain before she married Reg. The young ones also joined our tennis group.

My life changed that day at tennis in 1944, when Cliff asked me if I was interested in a position as a Baker-Pastry Cook.

At this time the Japanese were bombing Darwin. My dad said the Japanese were 'coming down', there was nothing really to stop them. We had already lost Singapore with thousands of men killed or captured.

Dad said, "People will always have to eat".

I was studying to become a doctor. All that went astray with my bakery apprenticeship. I continued with my career in the bread trade. If I hadn't, I probably wouldn't have met Rosalyn again. We were both in the Methodist Sunday school class together, but Rosalyn left when she turned 14.

I went on to become a Sunday School Teacher. We had Miss Jessie Condie as our Superintendent Teacher. *

I liked all the Harrys the first time I met them, and they liked me. I packed my clothes to start work and now that I was employed in Essential Services, I could go and buy tyres for my poor old push bike. I hadn't had any new tyres and tubes since 1939.

My bike

My first job! For the next 2 years, I had to call into Gerard & Sullivan - Butchers, who were next to Harry's town shop and pick up 2lb (0.9kg) of mince for the two trays of Sausage Rolls I had to make each morning. Not a soul on the streets at 6.30am, except for each Tuesday and Thursday when I passed Mr Bonnick and his off-sider, sitting on the running board of their night-soil truck — having their breakfast. I used to say 'Good Morning Mr Bonnick', and he always answered, 'Good Morning Son'.

At that time, bakers still started work at 7am. The sausage rolls had to go into No2 oven at 8.30am as soon as Cliff had room for them near the fire box. They had to be on the first delivery to the town shop. The carters, Steve and Henry ("the professor" as we called him), also started work at 7 am. Steve Heilbronn had a 1938 Morris Van, and the professor had Col (a beautiful ex racehorse) for his deliveries.

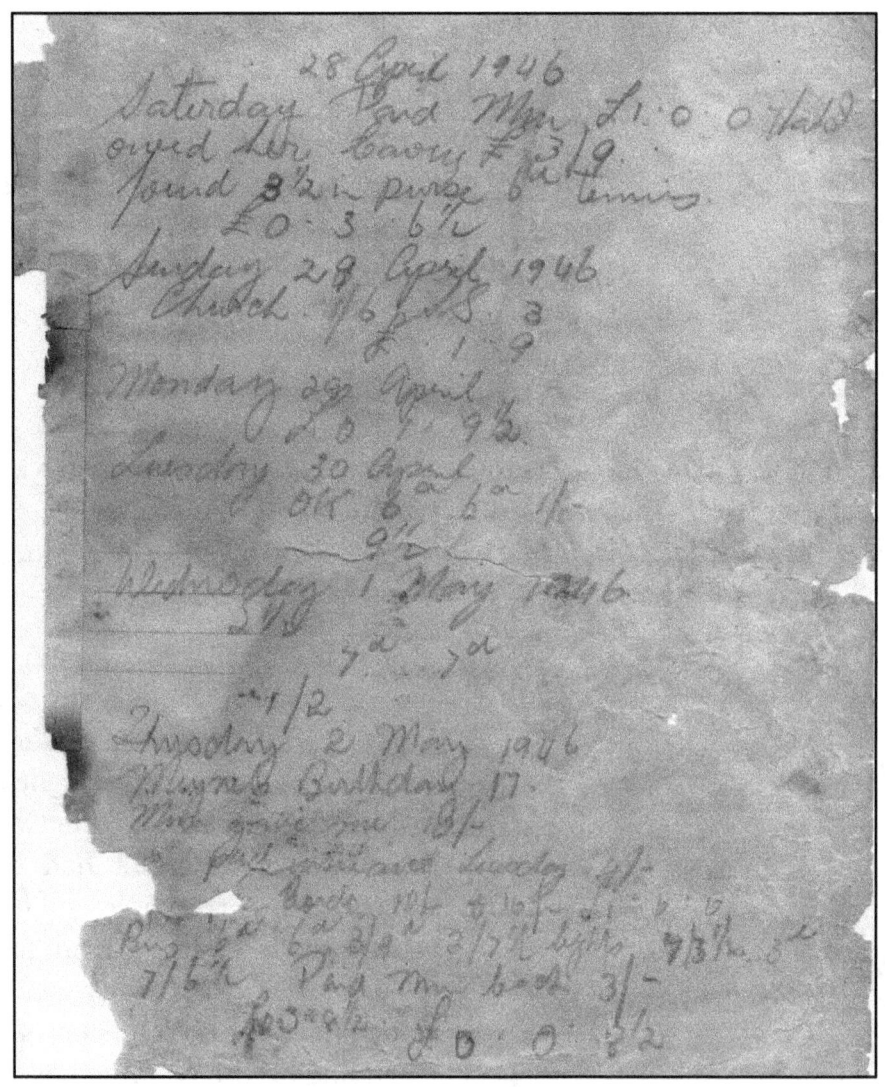

A page from my budget book - 1946

*I can still hear the jingle of the harness and chains as I was preparing two trays of sausage rolls to be cooked as soon as we could fit them into the first available empty space in the oven *.*

The only morning of the week they had hot bread delivery was on Mondays, the rest of the week the first delivery run was cold bread. The last bread out of the oven was placed into a closed cupboard awaiting delivery the next day. Carters always had Thursday's off in lieu of Saturday, when they did a full day's delivery. Bread was always available on Thursdays at the town shop and the bakehouse.

I was settling into my 19/6p ($1.95) for a 48 hour plus week. No such thing as overtime. You worked till the workload was completed. I gave ten shillings of my pay to my Mum for board, leaving 9/6p (95c) to clothe and pay for all my living expenses.

I had left high school unprepared for work. A tailor-made three-piece suit was £3/7/6p ($6.75)*.

I had cardboard in my shoes to keep the water out for many months before I could afford a new pair.

We were all very happy. Weekly sales were an average of 6000 loaves a week, dependent on the weather. Cold, wet days people ate bread with their soup, summer they ate more salads. Harrys brought in a larger variety of cake and biscuits. Because of the rationing of sugar and butter, there weren't any biscuits, like Arnott's, Vetoy, or Websters in the grocery stores. They were all made for the armed forces. Being an essential service, we weren't severely rationed, so Harry's made ginger nuts by the millions, all hand cut, one at a time.

Harry's also employed Hilda Moore as their shop girl. *Hilda's married name is Kidd and she lives at 39 Duke Street*.

Ted Priddy was No1 oven man. Cliff Harry was No2 oven man. Colin McBride was the other bakery apprentice and jobber for Ted Priddy.

When we visited the Bunya Mountains with our 'now grown' family, Rosalyn and I used to call in to see Betty and Colin at Kingaroy.

John Stark 15-16yrs in front of Harry's Bakery

John Stark, Colin McBride 2020

I was employed as baker pastrycook apprentice and was the jobber for Cliff Harry on oven $^{No}2$. I personally did many hours of unpaid overtime as we really did not start on the cakes and pastries till all the bread was nearly finished. Mr. Reg Harry spent a lot of time showing me things and explaining what went where and so forth.

On a Saturday morning in August, after the town shop had closed, Mr. and Mrs. Reg Harry and Elaine set forth to Brisbane, to visit Mrs Harry's mother, Mrs Rooney, in Toowong.

On the following Tuesday morning around 11am, Ted received an urgent message saying that his father had passed away from a massive heart attack. He was just 42 years of age.

Ted, Cliff & Beryl left for Brisbane immediately, leaving no one in charge in Gympie. We said no trouble, we will manage. What a mouthful! Three staff down. Neither Colin nor I had ever driven a car! But you know what? We loaded the Bedford and Col drove the delivery into the town shop and I drove it back to the bakehouse. We broke regulations for the next few days and started work at 5 am and I even did some cake baking, not much, just plain 'pattycakes' and scones. On the 2nd morning, they even had the sausage rolls. I think that the responsibility and sadness of those few days ... taught us a lesson that we took forward for life.

Mr Reg Harry was buried in the Toowong Cemetery. They all came home to Gympie after the funeral including Mrs Rooney. It was the only time I ever met Robert Harry and I never saw him again. He never married and came to Gympie to retire and is buried in the Gympie cemetery.

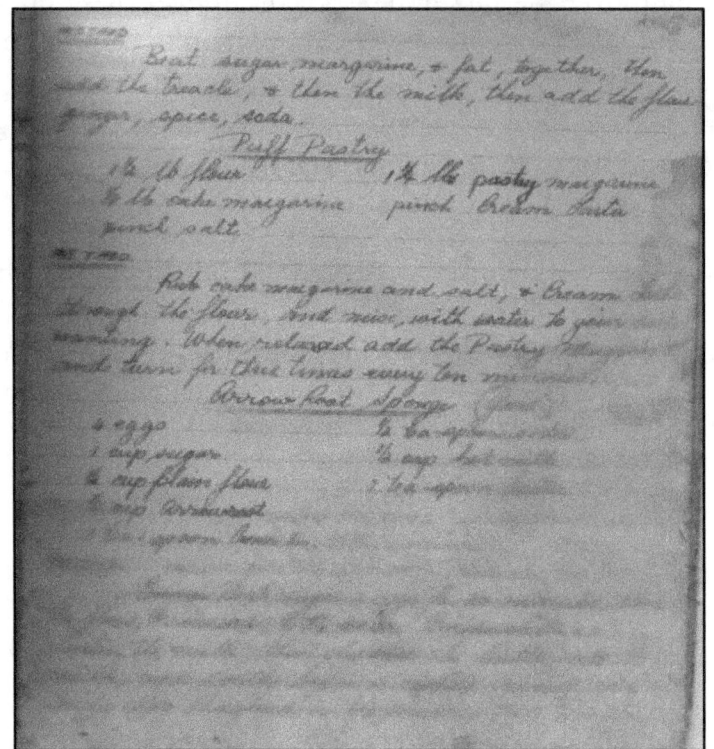

Page from my personal recipe book - 1946

Front Cover - Pilot Recipe Book 1945 *Inside Front Cover 1945*

INDEX

	Page
Baking Powder	1
" Temperatures	2
Cheap Cakes	3
Common Causes of Faulty Cakes	4
Weights and Measures	5

RECIPES

	Page
Afghans	6
Anzac Cakes	7
Apple Charlotte	8
" Squares	9
Banana Cake	10
Banbury Cakes	11
Biscuit Cake	12
Biscuits, Butter	13
" Chocolate Viennese	14
" Viennese	15
Block Cake—	
No. 1, Good Quality Fruit	16
No. 2, Good Quality Fruit	17
No. 3, Good Quality Fruit	18
No. 4, Medium Quality Fruit	19
No. 5, Light Fruit	20
No. 6, Cheap Quality Fruit	21
No. 7, Sultana	22
No. 8, Sultana	23
No. 9, Sultana	24
No. 10, Crumb	25
No. 11, Plain	26
Brandy Snaps	27
Bread, Chefel for use in	28
" Mixed Fruit	28
Buns, Hot Cross (Straight Dough)	29
" Piping Dough	30
" Lemon and Orange	31
" Raspberry	32
Burgundy or Honey Roll	33
Cheese Straws	34
Chefel in Bread Mixings	35
Chester Cake	36

	Page
Chocolate Cup Cakes	37
" Marshmallow	38
" Wheel Shorts	38
Christmas Pudding	39
Cinnamon Scrolls	40
Coconut Raspberry Slices	41
" Shorts	42
Coffee Drops	43
Cream, Mock—	
No. 1	44
No. 2	45
No. 3	46
No. 4	47
No. 5	48
No. 6	49
No. 7	50
No. 8	51
No. 9	52
No. 10	53
Cream or Custard Puffs	54
Crunchies	55
Cup Cakes or Trilbys	56
" Chocolate	57
Custard Slices	57
Date Cake, Canadian	58
" Loaf	59
French Drops or Kisses	60
" Pastry	60
Fruit Flans	61
" Flavoured Fillings	62
" or Nut Loaf	62
" Slices	63
Ginger Bread	64
" Gems	65
" Loaf	66
Honey Ginger Kisses	67
" or Burgundy Roll	33
Icing, Christmas Cake	68
" Royal	69
" Soft Dough	70
" Syrup for	71
Jelly Slices	72

	Page
Lamingtons	73
Lemon Cheese	74
" Cups	75
Macaroons, Almond	76
" Coconut	77
Madeira Cakes	78
Marshmallow	79
" Chocolate	80
Matches or Vanilla Slices	133
Meringues	81
Meringues, Boiled	82
Napoleon Ice Cakes	83
Nut Crumb Sheet	84
" Flake Crunchies	85
" Fingers	86
" or Fruit Loaf	62
Orange Cakes	88
Oyster Patties	89
Paste, Flaky	90
" Puff	91
" Short, Good Quality	92
" Short, Standard Quality	93
Pastry, French	94
Pies, Meat	95
" Meat for	96
" Mince	97
" Pumpkin	98
" Raisin	99
Piklets	100
Queen Drops	101
Raisin Sheet	102
Rock Cakes	103

	Page
Rollettes	104
Russian Cake	105
Salmon Patties	106
Sausage Rolls	107
Scone Flour	108
Scones	109
" Cream	110
" Pumpkin	111
" Vanilla	112
Short Bread	113
Sponge, Rich	114
" Good Quality	115
" Cheap Quality	116
" Fingers and Kisses	117
" Chocolate or Roll	118
" Rollettes	104
Tarts, Almond	119
" Chocolate Custard	120
" Coconut Custard	121
" Coconut	122
" Congress	123
" Coconut Cheese	124
" Crumb Cheese	125
" Custard	126
" Mince Fruit	127
" Neinish	128
" Sago Fruit	129
" Sherry Fruit	130
" Short Bread	131
" Sultana Viennese	132
Vanilla Slices or Matches	133

Index of Pilot Recipe Book – 1944 - 1948

Chapter 16

Harry Brothers – Bakers and Pastry Cooks
72-74 Duke Street Gympie
1945-1952

With the death of their father, Reg, the Harry boys, Ted and his younger brother Cliff, were now thrown into management. Ted had been in partnership with his dad from the purchase of the bakery, although his name wasn't included on the signs. Reg might have had a prelude of what was to come. Ted had already sold a very viable bakehouse at Home Hill.

I started my trade under Mr. Reg Harry, and after the boys returned from the funeral, things began to change. The business name changed to Harry Brothers and my apprenticeship was transferred to them.

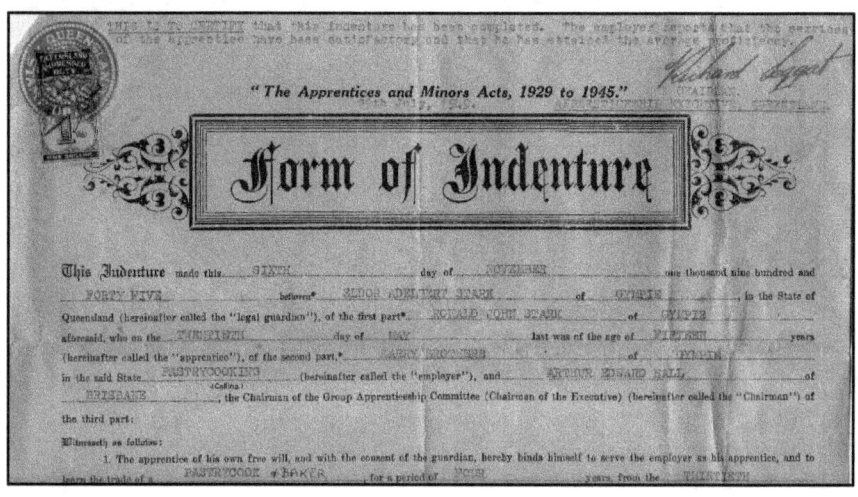

John Stark's Apprentice Papers - 1945

Ted started to keep company with a lovely lady named Joyce. We all met her one day at work. Ted disappeared quite a few nights, but we knew where to find him if he was needed. I liked Joyce very much. They were married about 8 months later and moved into the four-bedroom home next door with Mrs Harry senior.

Mrs Harry snr's home had an open verandah on the front and one side. On the front was hung green wooden blinds and Eileen

(Reg's youngest daughter) slept out there. The rear of the home had the bathroom on one corner and the kitchen on the other. In between the two rooms the verandah had been closed in with

The Harry's home. – Photo 2018

casement windows, allowing the space to be used as a long dining room with the back landing and external stairs coming off it.

Underneath the home, 320 bags, or 15 ton of flour was stored, practically covering all the cemented area. The office was in the front section of the underneath area, opening onto the 8' (2.43m) wide cobblestone breezeway between the home and the bakehouse. The horses in harness would be led along this breezeway each delivery day.

Every second morning, a little old man named Mr Holland, from Clematis Street, would shuffle past my open push out window as I made the sausage rolls. He came to pick up his quarter loaf of bread, so he did not have to pay delivery. He used to be wearing his slippers and they always were sopping wet with him cutting across the horse paddock.

Ted Priddy once told me of an old Gentleman who would come into the bakehouse on our cold winter mornings. He wore an old army uniform and one of those heavy World War 1 army overcoats. He always slept in Mrs Cox's grocery store tapered doorway. He would come into the bakehouse about 6.30 am. He had wet himself and Ted would open the ash pan doors and he would stand flopping his loose-fitting pants till they were dry, asking "cup of tea please", "cup of tea please" and of course Ted would see that he also had something to eat. Doug continued on with this good deed in 1947. We never asked his name, although I think Ted called him Alan. We never saw him again after that year. Where he came from each year, or where he went, who knows!

In my Air Training Corp. Uniform. Aged 16yrs

The war was at its worst, the Japanese seemed to be coming down our way, so I joined the Air Training Corp, my dad was the Squadron leader. We used to meet each Tuesday night at the Central Girls School (that full story was told in my first book *The War in Gympie 1939-1945*). All the lights around Gympie were covered. No street lights. We had two push-up windows in the new section of the bakehouse painted black, they hadn't been opened for years. In my section of workspace, my push out window was solid timber. The open window plus the doorway was all the light I had.

The wall of the building, first built by Henry Long in 1909, was 12" (30mm) thick, with only a door and two push out windows for light and air, it must have been hellishly hot with the internal ovens, though it wasn't much better with right hand firing ovens.

We were not to show any light from the building, so we were restricted to one 40-watt bulb hanging in each room. Just as well the doughs were white, we could hardly see each other when we arrived each morning.

I remember one pitch black, cold winter's morning when I arrived on my bike for work at 6am. I had picked up the mince for my sausage rolls and I walked across the carter's area to be met by a very large tarp ... or so I thought. It was about 12' (3.6m) across. On entering the bakehouse, I realised it was not a tarp but the first dough which the dough man (Stan Blakeway) had cast out.

On top of the mixer was a special spot to put the glass thermometer so that we could have a constant reading of the temperature of water and flour. Unfortunately, Bill had accidentally dropped the thermometer into the mixer. Glass and flour do not mix!!

The timber contractor, Bill Blackman, arrived around 7am to pick up the bread for his timber cutters, walked right across the dough and said to me "nice thick tarp you have out there". I didn't enlighten him as to what it was. This was the only time I ever heard of dough thrown out due to a broken glass thermometer in our bakery.

That afternoon we had an extra job before we went home. The dough was cut into pieces with shovels, loaded into the back of the Bedford panel van and off to Bonnick's paddock out past the cemetery. We could not handle the dough because of the broken glass. The wild animals would have had a feast on it. I hoped the glass didn't cause any loss of life.

In August 1945, the great news came over the ABC that the war was over. Cliff, Colin, and I jumped into the 1938 Morris utility. Cliff drove Colin and I in the back of the ute. I had picked up two empty four-gallon (18L) jam tins along with two long pieces of wood as we ran to the ute. We headed off down Duke Street towards Mary Street banging on the jam tins and yelling at the top of our voices "THE WAR IS OVER". People came running out, laughing, and waving.

We went right through the main street to the five ways, turned around at the silent cop and drove back down the main street again, yelling. For my deed, I received a bad gash on my left thumb from the lid of the jam tin, blood was covering my hand as I waived and yelled. When we arrived back at the bakehouse Joyce Harry cleaned and bandaged it up tight.

Not that night, but the next, streetlights came back on. Oh boy! many did not function after four years of not working and it took many weeks to repair them.

The Gympie City Electric Light Company only had a few older men keeping the DC flowing. Nothing had been renewed and nothing had been added to the department since 1939. The two wood fired steam boilers spinning the generators, were just limping along for three shifts a day. Two Submarine Diesel Engines were added to help them and about 18 months later, they changed over to AC power. The night sky lit up like a dream. The steam boilers went on working as stand ins for another two years, with Eric Brady supplying the cord wood.

All the homes and businesses scraped off the tape or took down the sheets that were criss-crossed over their windows and glass doors (done to prevent flying glass if the Japanese ever flew a bombing raid over Gympie).

The troops were coming home. Sadly, many of the young men were now only a dream, lost in war.

Harry's had big problems. Our old bakehouse had been wired for DC power. It would knock you flying away from the electricity but would not kill you. This old current was rubber covered copper wire, thread through a conduit metal pipe. At all corners the conduit had parted and rubbed the copper wire bare. When you reached for your wooden 'peel' (the instrument to fill and empty bread tins from your oven; the exact same tool is used today with wood fired pizza ovens, though probably made of aluminium,) you sometimes knocked these pipes and sparks would go everywhere.

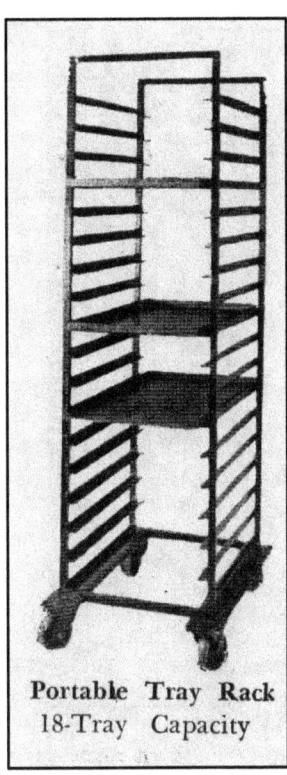

Portable Tray Rack
18-Tray Capacity

I remember when we carried our trays in the bun trolley. It was 6' (1.8m) high x 2' (0.6m) wide x 4' (1.2m) long and carried 18 trays of buns or coffee rolls to the proving box cupboard, which was to the right as you entered the bakehouse. We passed by the electric light switch for the two lights in the bakehouse. The switch was 5' (1.5m) high from the floor and made of this new stuff called Bakelite. If you cut your path a little too much to the right, the bun trolley would sheer off the switch. I once ended up on top of the nearest trough, shaking my head. I never had this happen again.

We had to be very careful with this new AC power, it would hold you to the wire; your muscles would contract, killing you.

The Harry boys had to have a quick job done to rewire the bakehouse. This time, they put a heat proof light on each oven door. These allowed us to see into the oven beautifully. A big difference from the 'dripping' lights we had a quite a few years before.

It was a big job changing the motors on the mixers, rollers, and cake machines to AC power and thankfully, all paid for by the Queensland Government.

I loved my work. Though I preferred Ted giving me my list of cake making for the day. He gave the list all in bulk lots. Not so Cliff, he gave me countless amounts of small orders. They took a lot longer to make, having to halve or quarter the recipes. On those days I arrived home closer to 6 p.m. The Harry Brothers wanted me to know as much as possible about pastry-cooking.

When I was 16, they sent me to the Gympie School of Arts to do a Cake Icing course. This kept me busy for two hours every Tuesday night for 12 weeks. I was the only male among 16

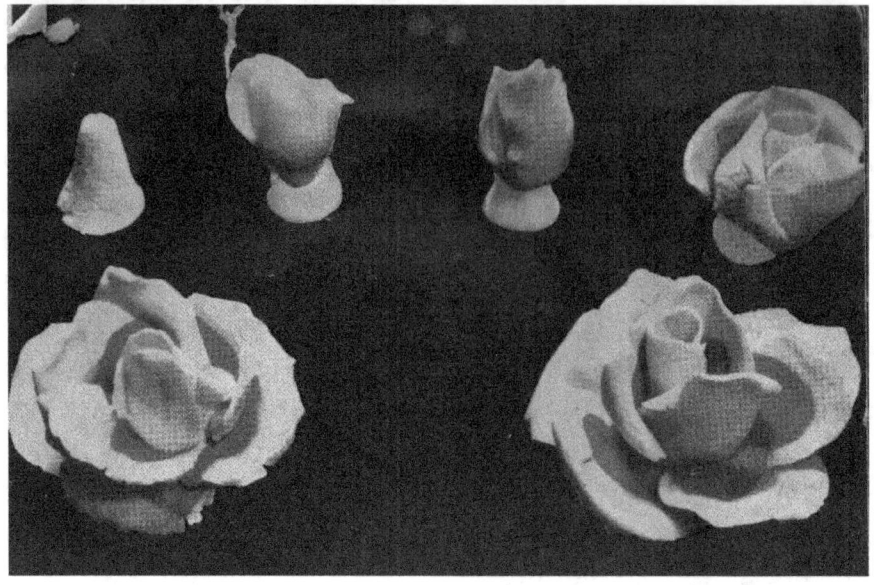

Rose Modelling

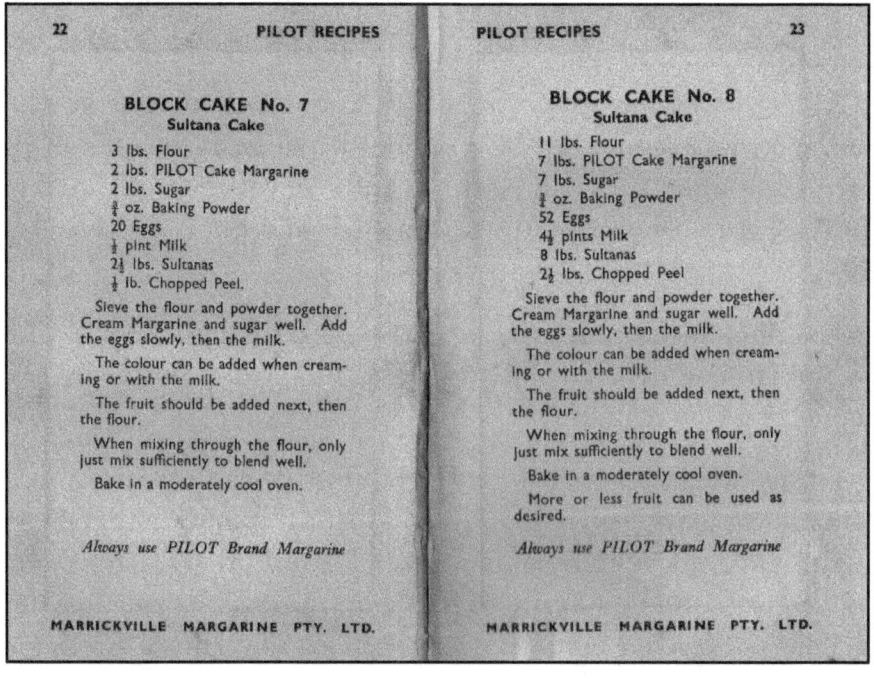

Sultana Cake Recipes I often used.

young ladies. When I first walked into the room with my cap and apron you could've heard a pin drop. After two weeks they couldn't help me enough with suggestions. I passed with flying colours.

A lady came into the bakery one morning and placed an order with Ted for an iced birthday cake with special wording on the top and to be ready in two days' time. Ted walked into the bakery and said to me. "I have a job for you, seeing you are now our 'main' cake icer. I had already made a supply of sultana light block cake a few days before, so, I was halfway there. I finished icing the cake the next day and thought I'd done a great job.

The lady arrived to pick up her cake after lunch on Thursday. I was working on small cakes, only 6' (1.8m) away. She looked at the cake and excitedly said "What a beautiful job, just what I wanted". Ted replied, "We always do a lovely job; in all we produce". The lady very happily agreed with Ted. I expected Ted to turn around and let the lady know that I was the one who had done her lovely cake. He thanked her for her payment and she, very excitedly, left the shop. I expected a large pat on the back, at the very least a "good job, John" from Ted, but not a word. I had just learnt a lesson. I was a 'cog in the wheel'.

On my retirement back to Gympie in May 1983, I noticed a name change on the old School of Arts. I went in and found it was now an Art Gallery. All the main internal walls had been removed allowing for large displays. I stood where my desk used to be and remembered. All the while telling the staff of 'the good old days. But I never forgot the lesson I learnt that day in the bakehouse many, many years before.

Always give credit, where credit is due.

One day, late in March 1946, around 3pm, two beautiful French Tourers with chrome spoked wheels pulled up outside on the driveway to our bakery.

Eight ladies and two older gentlemen alighted. I thought they were nuns at first, but I think two ladies carried babies. The men drove and they looked like they were Grandfathers. The ladies were dressed in long black dresses completely covering them from the neck to the ground and long sleeves to the wrists. They were all chatting and disappeared into Mrs Cox's shop. Mim and Mrs Cox were on duty that day.

About 20 minutes later as I was working on sponge rolls, I was suddenly surrounded by the eight women. They spoke so lovely. I was taken in and gave them free run of the bakery. When the old grandmother asked if she could bless the till, I suddenly realized they were Gypsies.

Our till was an old 2lb (0.9kg) jam tin, hiding on top of the full jam tins on a shelf above the door. I never looked in the direction of our hiding place; not once.

They took loaves of yesterday's and today's bread, buns and some Chester cake. They seemed to be everywhere and helped themselves to what they wanted. I tried to keep my eye on the eight of them, but goodness knows what they got up to. They finally left with what they had collected, worth a lot more than the 2/-(20c) they left on my work bench.

They all squeezed back into the two tourers. They had ports and boxes strapped onto the steel carriers at the back of each car. Bags of goods strapped to the running boards, beside the spare tyres. The canopies were folded back, open to all the dust on dirt roads. The engines were so quiet you could hardly hear them. I wondered how the grocery store handled the eight ladies and the Red Lion Service Station two doors up from the bakery. But I never thought to ask them.

When Mrs. Harry and Ted returned to the bakery after they had closed the town shop, I told them all that had happened.

I had never heard so much laughter from those two and they thanked me for not looking in the direction of the cash tin or giving them change.

Mrs Harry said that they often ask for change of 5/-(50c), so they could see where the till was located. Even if you just looked in the direction of its hiding place, let alone go to it, they seem to know.

Harry's Town Shop until 1968

My dad had previously told me all about the Gypsies of Europe. When I returned home that night, I told Mum and Dad of my experience. I remember years before, the Police visited their poultry farm on Wotton Hill, telling them to place guards on the chook runs because car loads of gypsies had left Cooroy heading for Gympie.

When I was working for Nudgee Bakery in 1957, my baker offsider was on his yearly two week's holiday and visiting his brother's property in northern New South Wales. He was driving back to the farm after doing some errands in the nearest town when he was flagged down by a pretty girl standing beside her holden ute and holding a can. He stopped and exchanged his full gallon tin which he kept behind the seat (those days, we all carried extra fuel if the need arose).

She assured him she could transfer the fuel, but no! Allen was the 'knight in shining armour' and took his time in transferring the fuel for her. She thanked him ever so much for stopping and he continued on to his brother's farm. When he arrived, he noticed his petrol gauge showed nearly empty. Also missing, were his brothers six piglets that were supposed to be under the cover in the back of the ute.

They reported all this to the local police, who informed them that gypsies were in the district and to please be careful.

The police said that her brothers were probably down beside the road waiting and swung into action emptying Alan's tank while he so kindly filled hers. The police had no answer on how they kept the piglets quiet. There wasn't any blood on the floor either.

Allan told us all about his adventure when he returned to work, and I told them all about my experiences with the gypsies at Harry Brothers in Gympie.

My dad told me that Gypsies can enter a chook yard so stealthily and remove the birds without a squeak from them.

In the war years everyone was on rations and coupons. Because I was working in an essential service, I received one gallon of petrol one month and two gallons the second month from the Government for my 1939 Coventry Eagle.

Ted and Cliff always had a spare coupon or two for Colin and me. We could not travel any distance, as the roads were practically impassable. The army trucks and tanks had cut up all the roads across the State and I needed the fuel to get to work.

Harry Brothers always joined in all sorts of community projects. Like the year that the Bedford van was done up as a loaf of brown bread in a procession down Mary Street. The canvas canopy was folded back far enough to allow us to cut a hole in the top of the bread so I could throw brown paper bags with little sausage rolls inside to the onlookers. I also threw out little cupcakes in white paper bags. I poked my head out of the hole at one point and out of the crowd rang the words "STARK, THE BIG WEEVIL". Everyone roared with laughter.

Another year we were sitting on top two chairs welded to the spars of the Bedford van roof. Colin McBride, dressed by Beryl Harry as a beautiful Bride, he wore two oranges in the bra as padding and Col really looked the part. I was the bridegroom. Everybody kept asking me, "Who was my Bride"?

Another time, Ted Harry was dressed up as a staunch Methodist Lady, again by his sister Beryl, and this time I was a Methodist Minister with collar and all. On our way home we dropped into Thelma Hayes 21st birthday party held at her parent's home. We introduced ourselves as Reverend and Mrs Herbert McGillacutty. We had them all fooled! We stayed for about twenty minutes, ad-libbing the whole time. What a show we put on for them! At church the following day the party goers had worked out that it was me masquerading as the Reverend, but we never let on who was playing the part of my wife.

Cliff, while a member of our church choir, met and courted a lovely young lady by the name of Glen Wyllie. They were married two years later. Cliff was a beautiful tenor and had previously won Australian Amateur Hour in 1946.

From Left: John Stark, Ted Harry, Cliff Harry, Glen Harry (nee Wyllie), Joan Wyllie, Beryl Harry, and Maureen Hallett. Photo 1947

In the above wedding photo, the photographer had me sit down as I was a head taller than Cliff or Ted. Their brother Robert was to arrive from Mount Isa to be groomsman, but he never arrived. I wasn't told why, just asked to fill in for him.

The wedding celebration finished at the Gympie Railway Station when their guests put Glen and Cliff onto the 11:30pm Sunshine Express steam train bound for Cairns.

They were in a carriage complete with sleeping accommodation ... but sharing with two other couples. They all sat up for the two and a half days it took to get to Cairns.

Ted, Colin, Cliff, Glen, and I all became members of Gympie's "Pop Anderson's" Choir.

The bakehouse became our rehearsal hall, and we practiced every day. We were in plays, Eisteddfod's and of course in the Methodist Church Choir. You name it and we were there and having a ball in each other's company.

We were asked by the Army Cooks stationed at the Gympie Showgrounds to make one batch of Army dog biscuits, made to their recipe, three inches square and tasteless. But, with bully beef, it kept our troops alive.

Harrys were always trying to improve the quality of their bread and cake. Now that the war was over, the restrictions were lifted, and they could purchase flour from any mill. They bought their flour from eight different Flour Mills.

- Seafoam Flour Mill, Stanley Street, South Brisbane.
- Commonwealth Flour Mill, Stanley Street, South Brisbane.
- Gillespie's (Anchor Brand) Flour Mill, Albion Brisbane.
- Silverspray Flour Mill, Maryborough, Queensland. Manager: - Mr. Buckberry.
- Warwick Flour Mill, Warwick Queensland.
  Local Rep: - Mr. Garrick.

- Toowoomba Flour Mill (Defiance Brand), Toowoomba, Queensland.
- Dalby Flour Mill, Dalby, Queensland: and
- Barnes Milling Company, Stanley Street, Brisbane.

Harrys and I chose the flour from the Warwick Mill as the best performance flour. I was told this was because it was a harder grain of wheat.

Nowadays, only Defiance Flour is still producing. The other mills are gone.

When I had the Amamoor Bakery, I kept an empty flour bag from each Mill that I purchased from and have them in my Bakery Collection. I have shown this collection to organisations that have invited me over the years to speak on my days as a Baker-Pastry Cook. In my collection I have caps, aprons, bread tins and recipe books.

There was great excitement and panic one Wednesday afternoon. Ted, Cliff, and I were doing pastry work when Col the horse came galloping into the loading bay. He was in a lather of sweat from head to tail. We calmed him down and looked around for Tom Bradley, the carter. He was nowhere to be seen. Next question! Did Tom have an accident? About 20 minutes later the telephone rang, it was Tom, way out at Alans at Chatsworth, some 5 miles out of town. Tom said that a strange noise had startled the horse while he had his head in the back door of the cart. Alans was the nearest phone where he could ring from. Tom said the last he saw of the horse and cart was Col in full gallop on the highway heading for Gympie.

Petrol, along with clothing, sugar, tea, and butter was still only available on Ration Card and luckily, nothing was travelling on the highway that day.

Every year, poultry farmers sold their eggs in two seasons. The laying season, when the price of eggs went down cheap at 1/- (10c) per dozen and the moulting season when the price of eggs went through the roof, up to 1/6p (15c) per dozen. So, our egg supply was either a flood or a famine.

Ted and Cliff had been talking to the Egg Marketing Board (EMB) about this problem and were told of newly discovered way to preserve eggs by water glaze.

Ted and Cliff purchased 20 clean 44-gallon drums with clip on lids from Shell Oil and stored them under the house. (With the war over and regular deliveries restored we didn't need to carry such a huge stock of flour anymore). As per the instructions, we half-filled the drums with water, added the correct amount of salt and the keeping agent purchased from the EMB.

Thousands of eggs were bought in the 'plenty' months and added to the drums. We closed the drums down and waited for the lean supply months to arrive. Mind you, we used hundreds of eggs every day when we were making cakes. 40 to 60 eggs in some recipes.

Finally, it came time to start using our preserved eggs. Cliff told me to use the eggs from the first drums, which I did. I opened the first drum to find a few rotten eggs floating in the liquid. That was okay, we could afford to lose a _few_ eggs. All went well until one morning some weeks later, when I lifted the lid off a new drum. The rotten egg stench nearly knocked me down. Some of the eggs had broken and the rest had floated, which made the eggs unusable.

One afternoon later that week I was down the back paddock, getting my oven timber loaded on to the trolley for the next day's firing, when WHOOSH!!! and a terrible smell of rotten eggs. Colin had loaded about 20 of the rotten eggs onto the edge of the underground water tank and was trying to hit me with them ... and me desperately trying to avoid getting hit. Of course, when Colin was at the woodheap getting his supply of oven timber it was his turn to avoid the rotten eggs.

This went on every day for about a week, by then we had worked out to stand a sheet of galvanized iron to hide behind, that is, until Mrs Harry snr. looked out of her dining room window and saw what was going on ... it stopped immediately.

In the following days, Colin and I had to drain the excess water from the remaining drums with eggs exploding with the movement of the drums, we loaded four drums at a time into the back of the Morris utility and made the trip out to Bonnick's paddock. The same paddock where three years prior, we had emptied the glass contaminated dough.

We found out from talking to the EMB, that each of these drums were only supposed to take about 20 dozen eggs. If you loaded more, the weight of the eggs would crush the bottom ones making the water glazes unusable. A very expensive lesson was learnt. We estimated each drum had contained at least 40 or 50 dozen eggs.

In the future, Harry Bros bought all their eggs in pulp. All our recipes had to be converted to egg weight instead of egg number. The EMB supplied us with fresh egg pulp each week.

In late 1944, Wren was transferred to Gympie PMG to be one of my dad's team leaders. Wren and Mrs Jensen brought their three daughters Joan, Beryl, and Alma with them and moved into the private upstairs unit above the Cox's Grocery Store, next door to the bakehouse. Beryl came to work for Harry Brothers in their office under the house.

Beryl Jensen worked the same hours as the carters, so she could handle the accounts. Nearly all customers would book up their purchases each month. Beryl married late in life to Ray Heilbronn. June married, but Cancer took her at an early age and Alma married one of my old school mates, Dudley Groundwater, and had one son.

In 2020, Alma lives alone on the south side of Gympie. Dudley had passed away in 2016.

Every few days, a beautiful girl would walk past the bakehouse to the grocery store next door and as she was passing, she would give me a little wave and say "Hello, John". At that time, I had a girlfriend in Greenslopes, Brisbane, but this young Gympie lady she seemed to know me. Well, nobody seemed to know her, I finally asked the bread carter, Tom Bradley, and he said she was Pop Pritchard's daughter, Rosalyn.

Every Monday morning Mr Pritchard, a timber contractor, would call in to pick up eight loaves of bread for his timber cutters.

Strangely, I had not seemed to notice this beautiful girl as she grew into a young lady. She had changed since our Sunday School days.

The weeks went by to the beginning of August. Rosalyn was on a visit to the grocery store and all the staff called out "Hello Ros". I had my head in a bowl mixing sponge cakes and I heard Col say to Doug that he was going to ask her out.

Now don't get me wrong, Col is a nice bloke and a great friend, just not the type I thought good enough for Rosalyn to know. I quickly wrote a rough note asking her to go to the pictures with me and giving it to Tom Bradley for him to pass onto Rosalyn when he delivered their bread the next day. I still have her reply letter tucked safely away, agreeing to accompany me, but first she wanted to introduce me to her Mum and Dad at dinner next Saturday night.

One morning, Ted told us that Doug Roy (staff from Clermont) was returning to us from the war to finish his apprenticeship as a baker pastry cook.

Doug had lied about his age and the level of his bakery training to enlist in the Army. After basic training he was sent to Dutch New Guinea. The Japanese had his unit pinned down on an airfield for 18 months. They were starved for fresh food. Aircraft could not land. The men would repair the runway and the Japanese would then shell it and destroy their work.

They lived on Bully Beef and powdered potatoes, dropped from Douglas DC3 aeroplanes. Doug had made an oven out of flat drums. Flat drums happened when parachutes did not open. He set them into an earth bank and lit internal fires, just like Wellers at Widgee Crossing in 1867. From the occasional dropped drums of flour, he made cob loaves. Occasionally the planes would drop powdered yeast and Doug was able to make bread. 140 men were in Doug's unit. He told me that when they were at last relieved at Port Moresby, they all got stuck into T-bone Steaks and dysentery set in, in a bad way.

It took twelve months to bring Doug back to full health after the war finished in 1945. He had been in hospital with a series of problems especially Malaria. He had also married his childhood sweetheart Betty.

At the end of 1946, Doug arrived back in Gympie to finish his trade with his previous employer, Reg Harry, but Reg had since passed away in 1945. Harry Brothers Bakery took over his apprenticeship and the Army paid for Doug's time to finish his trade.

Rented home of Doug & Betty Roy 1946. Photo 2018

Harry Bros. had rented them the home across the road in Duke Street. At odd times throughout the years Doug and I worked together.

Rosalyn and I became lifetime friends with Betty and Doug. Betty passed away in 1999 and Doug passed away in Cooinda Nursing Home on 23.3.2003.

The only sad part about Doug coming home was that he would become ⁿᵒ1 oven man. Ted Priddy had spent his whole working life at this bakehouse and being in his sixties was not quite ready for retirement. He left Harry Brothers on two weeks holiday, (that was all you received those days, no such thing as long service leave), and I am afraid he was also a little bitter.

He obtained a position with James Fardoolie and he used to drive his Rugby Tourer car past the Harry bakery each day on his way home. He never once looked in or waved to me.

In 1947, I traded my Coventry Eagle motor bike in and bought a used 1946 Royal Endfield from Superior Motor Bodyworks, the dealership for Gympie and District. That model was the first bike produced in England after the end of World War 2.

On the 20th of July 1947, Beryl Harry woke with pains, Mrs Harry rang Dr Lindsay, who came straightaway to their home. He stated she had Appendicitis' and rushed her direct to the Glandore Hospital where he operated on Beryl and in 2 weeks she returned home. I spoke to her a few times wishing her all the best. When, on the following Tuesday morning, Beryl awoke and was unable to open her mouth, they raced her back to Glandore. Beryl had developed Lockjaw and Dr Lindsay fought to keep her alive. Beryl died on the 13.9.1947. She was only 19 years of age and is buried in the Methodist section of the Gympie Cemetery. I visited her on occasions over the passing years. A lonely grave (you can feel it), among the graves from long lost past lives. I do hope that she is not forgotten by the families that she belonged to.

In 1948 I rode my motor bike from Chermside in Brisbane to Gympie on the highway. I passed seven vehicles. Three belonging to the Army and four private vehicles.

That year I also enlisted in the Australian Army for three years. My number was 1/32281. Sadly, I handed my notice in at Harry's.

I was courting Rosalyn at this time and failed to discuss this move with her. She cried but forgave me when I finished my basic training in Rockhampton and was stationed with the 42nd Infantry Battalion at the Gympie Drill Shed in Duke Street.

Private R.J. Stark
Army Number Q1/32281
Central Queensland Regiment
B Company 42nd Infantry Battalion
Stationed at Gympie Drill Shed, C.M.F.
Dispatch Rider (Donard) September 1948
Lend Lease U.S.A. Harley Davidson 1942
A.M.F. Number 61692 Regiment No. 169

Because the army only required us to work 3 days a week, I applied to work off base and was offered the choice of serving in Japan with the occupational forces or transferring into the reserves with the commitment of attending training nights and weekends. I chose the Reserves and looked for work.

I was offered a good pay rise to work for Di Reese in Nambour. £9/3/5d ($18.65) instead of the £4/8/- ($8.80) I had been receiving at Harry's. My mate, Alf Bowden, had also just been transferred to Penney's of Nambour (a white goods store).

I had only been working for Di for five weeks when I was doubled over with a terrible pain on my right side. A rush trip to Nambour Hospital and emergency surgery for acute appendicitis and having 12 weeks off work to recuperate. Di was again in desperate need of a baker, so he had to replace me, and I lost my position.

In those days, you could walk out of a job today and step into another tomorrow. I found work with Norm Searle of Beerburrum. Only 40 miles from Brisbane and no electricity, so it was back to handmade breads and cakes. Most of Norm's customers were forestry workers.

Rosalyn and Mrs Robinson had caught the Rockhampton Mail Steam Train. Rosalyn got off the train at Beerburrum to spend the day with me while Mrs Robinson travelled onto Brisbane to order dress stock. They had their return tickets for that night.

Norm and Bertha loved Rosalyn from the start. Rosalyn pleaded with me to return to Gympie. At the same time my father met with a cousin of ours, Bill Muller, known to all as Pop. As they were talking, he told dad of his General Store in Amamoor in The Mary Valley and of a bakehouse on the block next door, that had been closed since 1936.

Since my operation, I had applied for a discharge from the Army and seeing Australia wasn't at war, I was allowed to resign my commission. In the meantime, I contacted Ted Harry to see if they had any opening for me. Unfortunately, he had none, but a position was to become available with James Fardoolie.

I was going to take the place of Ted Priddy!!! he was retiring at last and if I wanted the position as No2 oven man with Billy Branch as my Jobber, it would be available in six weeks' time. I gave my notice to Norm, and they were both very upset when I told them I was returning to Gympie, though Rosalyn was over the moon.

Engagement photo 1948

I sold my motor bike to a forestry worker before moving back to Gympie and asking Mr and Mrs Pritchard for permission to be engaged to their eldest daughter, Rosalyn.

I asked Rosalyn to marry me and after she accepted, we went to John Balthes Jeweller of Mary Street, where I used a portion of the money made from the sale of my bike to buy the engagement ring. I told Rosalyn at this point I had no idea as to when we could be married. Rosalyn and I were over the moon and our families were drawn together. Both of our fathers were World War One veterans.

Rosalyn was a dressmaker and designer of distinction. She had her own business at the Fiveways, Gympie, with a staff of three.

*The only advertising that the Harry's ever did was the yearly calendars in 1947 and 1948.

The doors to Harry Brothers, Duke Street were closed in 1952 after Ted and Cliff Harry bought out W & J Condie and moved the business to 32-38 Reef Street.

The Supermarkets and Hot Bread Shops were slowly winning the customers.

2018 photo of 72-74 Duke St. Bakery of Henry Long, Bill Blakeway, Reg Harry & Harry Bros.

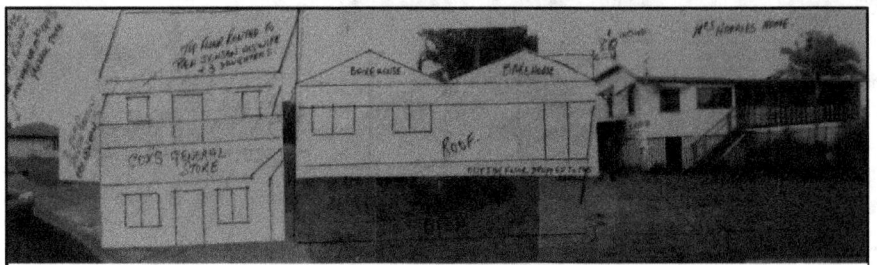

1887 to 1952 Mud Map of 68 - 74 Duke Street

Cliff and Glen Harry had six children Reg, Beryl, Trevor, Janine, Peter, and David. None of the children went into the bakery trade.

Chapter 17

James Fardoolie—Baker
5, 5a, 7 Apollonian Vale, Gympie.
1948-1968

James (Pop) Fardoolie purchased this bakery in April 1948 from the Sherran Family, who had returned to their own bakery at Sherwood, Brisbane. This bakery had been leased to Bernie McKenna.

Ross Sherran's home on allotment No5 was not included in the sale, as his cousin wished to purchase the property. that is; 74 years ago.

James arrived in Gympie and made himself known to all his opposition. He was of Greek Heritage. At first, his English was a little hard to understand.

The bakeries of Gympie still had in operation the set delivery areas the D^D had put into place in 1939. The system had worked well for the past nine years, and they all had agreed to continue with this system. So, James Fardoolie not only bought the bakery, he had also bought the bakeries delivery runs.

Billy Branch Photo 1938

James was n°1 oven man with David Collins as his Jobber, Ted Priddy was No2 oven man, his Jobber was Billy Branch (who stayed working in the premises of his family's bakehouse for all his working life). Gordon Hayes was his dough man. His two horse and cart bread carters were Billy Branch and Norm Ganley.

In the bakery, he had the huge dough machine that Isaac branch put in place and a Sterling Bread Moulder. Everything else was done by hand. He sold out of the shop in the front of the bakery, and he also had a very good delivery business to farmers via the Cream Carriers.

When I phoned James asking about the oven man's position to replace Ted Priddy, I informed him I could start at any time. He took me at my word and asked me to come in as soon as possible.

I was to do the doughmaking for two weeks, oh boy! the climbing up those steel stairs to that huge dough machine. **It was the noise.** I had just come from the quiet of handmade doughs at Beerburrum. The noise of that dough machine had not changed since Branch's days.

James was living in the home at No7, right next to the dough room wall and I could see he was not happy with the noise, especially in the early part of the night with the eight-hour doughs.

James Fardoolie's home built in the 1940's is behind the brick home

Big discussions were held to how he could build a new home out in the horse paddock. With two horses to accommodate, the stables would have to be relocated to the rear of the paddock. This in turn would mean less grass to night feed his horses, therefore more feed would have to be bought. But it also meant that when his new home was built, he then could sell the original Branch home at $^{No}7$. He set out in high hopes to be in his new home by next January, which he achieved.

When I arrived, Billy Branch welcomed me with open arms. It was a joy to discuss with him the old days when I was a young lad and used to visit the bakery with my father, a bread vendor, and me now returning 18 years later to work with Billy. He also knew Rosalyn, because his bread run had included her home until the 1939 D^D. division. Nothing was any trouble for Billy. He was a lovely man; I can still see his smiling face as he would race the hot bread away from my tipping point and stack it neatly in the movable stands. When I worked for Pop, his trade was around 1250 loaves a day.

While working for James in 1949, I had negotiated a deal with my cousin to re-open the Amamoor Bakery. I was still waiting for my discharge from the Army and still on extended furlough. My discharge did not come through until 20.1.1950.

I had told no one of my plans. I borrowed a motor bike from my friend, Viv Burton, who owned the Superior Motorbody Works in Stewart Terrace. The road to Amamoor was so bad I lost the complete section of back mudguard including the number plate and taillight. The most comfortable way to ride was to stand on the stirrups. When I re-opened Amamoor I bought a second-hand Chevrolet 1929 ute from Badson's in Mellor Street. Even driving the ute, the bad condition of the road made it hard to steer and keep my ute on the road. More of that story in chapter 18.*

As the years rolled by, trade was dropping dramatically, with the work force taking more women, nobody was at home to receive bread or pay for it. James found he did not require two bread carters anymore as one could safely cover his customers, so Norm Ganley was stood down.

In 1968 James approached Neil Rogers of Mothar Mountain Road to see if he was interested in taking over what small trade he had left. Neil had converted his Poultry & Egg Business into a Hot Bread Shop. James and Neil came to an agreement and James closed down his bakehouse.

He then sold the bakehouse for removal. Goodness knows where the Dough machine went! The Sterling bread rolling machine might have gone over to Neil Rogers.

James sold the bakehouse land; the new owners built a low set brick home. He then sold the back property.

The last I heard of James Fardoolie was that he may have retired to the Toowoomba area?

I lost track of Billy after he retired.

Our return to Gympie in 1983 and finding that nearly all my old friends had passed away, was a sad time of my life. Rosalyn and I should have called throughout the passing years and kept in touch, even making a phone call would have been nice, but with the raising of four beautiful children, all involved in Clubs and Church, the short visits to Rosalyn's parents and my sister, Joyce and Irv Runge, was as far as we ventured. We were too late for a lot of past friends.

I started to remember all the things that at one time were so important to me. The Central State School were soon to celebrate their 120-year anniversary and I was asked to write down memories of my Central School days. Five books of Gympie's history later, this will make number Six.

Chapter 18

John Stark-Baker, Pastry Cook
Busby Street, Amamoor, Mary Valley
1949-1952

I have told you small snippets of my life, as a child, a young man, now to be a businessman in the District of Gympie.

You have read of my Father's contact with our cousin Bill (Pop) Muller, owner of the General store at Amamoor and his telling my dad of the empty bakehouse, now used as a cattle and horse feed storage area.

I was interested in looking at this proposition. I discussed it fully with Rosalyn, the pros and cons! Would the Army finally give me my demob papers?

I had not even laid eyes on this property yet or seen what was still in the bakehouse. Was the oven still in usable condition? All this laid heavily on my mind and most importantly, when would Rosalyn and I be able to afford to be married.

Bill Muller could only guarantee sales to around 500 loaves maximum a week. At present, bread was supplied by Mr Bill Bullock, the baker from Kandanga, the next town up the Railway line in the Mary Valley. He also supplied bread to the second Grocery Store in Amamoor and the Currans General Store in Dagun, one town closer to Gympie.

The third General Store in Amamoor on the other side of the railway line had previously closed and was now converted into a family home.

My mind was in turmoil. I borrowed Viv Burton's motor bike on Monday, and after I finished work Tuesday lunch time, I travelled the dirt road to Amamoor to see what the future could possibly hold for Rosalyn and me.

As I pulled up at the general Store my first view was as this photo. *This store is not that much different today, 72 years later*.

Business Card 2018. Store no longer has bowsers out front.

Bill (Pop) Muller and his wife, Helen (my cousin), came out the door and down the three steps and shook my hand. A warm welcome as this was the first time I had met my cousins.

Then I looked across the yard to the wilderness that lay in front of the bakehouse, and to the shop which had been moved some 20' (6m) out onto the foot path.

Jimmy Chapple, a Gympie barber, came out and rented the shop each Wednesday afternoon. Jimmy had now stopped cutting hair here in Amamoor because he was too busy in Gympie.

Bill told me he had an old Boar War Veteran by the name of Stanley living in the single accommodation attached to the flour room. No electricity. No tanks, as both had rotted away many years before.

Can you imagine what was going through my mind and wondering what to expect when we prised open the door to the bakehouse? ... Well! it had about a dozen bags of chaff ... a lovely aroma. I slid the half cover off the top of the wooden trough. It was lined with Zincanneal, and except for a few knife holes in the bottom, was in very good condition.

I then turned my gaze towards the oven, the makers plate was as good as new. Thompson and Son Oven Makers, Gympie, Queensland. I didn't have a torch and without electricity when I opened the oven door all I could see was ... a black hole.

First look at Amamoor Bakery

The two work benches along both side walls were in reasonable condition. If needs be, I could turn the wooden tops over. There was nothing else in the bakery, no tins, no peels, but hanging down everywhere, were cobwebs. You could hardly see at all through the two windows.

Bill and Helen introduced their family to me, and I got to meet my other cousins. Lance, around 25 years and his wife, Fay, Roy, 22 years, Marie, 20 years, Laurie, 17 years and Helen, 14 years. Marie ran the Post Office. Helen was still attending Gympie High School and went into school on the 8:30am Rail Motor five days a week.

I thanked Bill and Helen and I left them with a lot on my mind. Like how was I going to pay for this complete outfitting? I had already sold my motor bike and used some of the money to buy my darling's engagement ring. Fardoolies were paying me, after tax, £9/4/- ($18.40c) a week as an ovens man. On the trip home over the rough road, I lost the mudguard with the pillion and number plate attached off the borrowed motorbike. I searched the roadside and gutters but wasn't able to find it. Another expense!

Many things flashed through my mind. The strong emotion to have my own bakery. To buy outright or lease a bakery was out of the question. If all went well with this idea of restarting the Amamoor bakery, we could be married, and Rosalyn and I wanted this so much. It became our driving force.

Only a few years before, Pfeffer's bakery at Kalbar in the

Rope Infected Bread

Fassifern Valley was offered to Dad and me. My parents grew up there, southwest of Ipswich, Queensland. I thought long and hard about it, the whole bakehouse would be on my shoulders.

We had also heard on the bakery grapevine that Pfeffer's Bakery was having trouble with 'rope' (a bacterial decomposition which leads to a peculiar slimy or ropy consistency on the inside of the loaf), that meant a lot of extra work in trying to clean it out with vinegar. We moved forward with caution, checking and re checking all facts. Dad never said a word, he left the decision to me. I declined the offer.

After arriving back in Gympie, that night we all sat down together, Mum, Dad, Rosalyn, and me to discuss what Amamoor had to offer us.

First, I would have to equip myself with a good torch, a dustpan and brush and a good seven strand straw broom, to clear the way. This would allow me to have a really good look at the overall property. So many things were flashing through my mind.

> **Summary**
>
> Bread should be always well baked, and soft sides on the bread should never be permitted. Well-baked bread is almost impervious to mould spores. It should be borne in mind that the common mould spores are destroyed in the oven, therefore any development of mould found on the bread is usually due to carelessness in permitting dust to accumulate where the freshly baked bread is stored. Always cool the bread, if practicable, by stacking in a shaded position until the steam has gone out of it; the bread should, therefore, not be stacked too close whilst hot.
>
> **Suggested Formula**
>
> 1 to 2 oz. of Acetic Acid or 1 quart of vinegar to each 150 lb. of flour is considered a safe and reliable means of delaying or preventing the development of mould, or use 2 to 4 oz. of "Salvin" to each 150 lb. of flour.
>
> **Conclusion**
>
> Briefly stated, even a severe outbreak of Rope and Mould in a Bakery can be quickly controlled by the liberal use of vinegar in the dough liquor and upon all bakehouse equipment; with an additional thorough cleaning after each day's work is completed. And always bake the bread thoroughly.
>
> 32

Official instructions to eradicate Rope from the bakery.

I said that I would be going out on Saturday afternoon with my borrowed cleaning tools. Rosalyn was very disappointed as she could not come with me this time. The Mary Valley Road was so bad, I was hoping no rain had fallen or I would have mud up all over me. That afternoon my young cousin, Laurie, helped me knock down all the cobwebs and move the bags of chaff into the flour room.

The following weekend, Rosalyn and her Mum and Dad drove me out in their New Austin A70 sedan. Dad drove very carefully on that crook road, especially through Long Flat, a well-known bog hole. They were impressed with my initiative but said very little. I had to make up my mind, it was all up to me. Would people like my bread? Would they like Rosalyn and I?

I was still not convinced to accept what Bill was offering me, and to give him the answer that he was waiting for.

The condition of the oven was my main concern. If repairs had to be done, it could cost more than I had. I called in on my parent's friend, Bill Thompson, who had built the oven in 1914, and on the following Saturday afternoon, Mr Thompson in his Bedford panel van, picked up Rosalyn and I, unfortunately, there wasn't room for my dad.

Bill came across when we arrived, and we gave the whole place a good going over.

Mr Thompson stated that the oven was in good condition. When he built the oven, he said 'he used about a ton of horseshoes and bits of steel, he found lying around the place, he placed all this in the soul (base) of the oven.

Previously, there had been a Blacksmiths shop and forge on this block. Cousin Bill could not give me any help with information on this.

Mr Thompson gave the all-clear for the oven, but first, I would have to climb into the oven, rake up and remove 1" (2.54c) of sand that had fallen down through the dry cracks in the curvature in the oven roof. Steam from the first load of baked bread would solve that problem.

In the week ahead I made a box with two ropes, to help me empty the oven of sand. One rope for me to pull the box into the oven and the other for my young cousin Laurie to drag the full box out after I had filled it with sand using a dustpan and brush. In the highest point of the oven, I only had 20" (50.8cm) to work in. The oven was 10' (3m) square and held around 150 loaves. Thank goodness I wasn't claustrophobic.

I also found out that another cousin, Merv Cooper, was the head of the Forestry and lived with his family in one of the three houses up at the big nursery. They also had married quarters and single men's barracks ... maybe another source for sales of my baked goods.

This forestry covered all the forest replanting of pine in the Imbil, Kandanga, and Amamoor area and the workforce consisted of men and women from all parts of Europe. England, Germany, Greece, Yugoslavia, Romania, France, Italy, Holland, Denmark, and Sweden. They came from so many different countries. There were Doctors, Dentists, Accountants, Engineers, Housewives, and Families. To immigrate here they had to give Australia two years of falling scrub and hand planting thousands of acres of pine trees.

We sure did have trouble understanding each other at first! But they all persisted with the schooling of English at night, and we soon became good friends.

The workers were paid full wages and accommodation while they worked for the Forestry. After they had worked their two years, they were then allowed to enter the Australian workforce if they wished. A lot stayed working with the Forestry.

I arranged to come out on Sunday, my mind was still all up in the air. I had put out feelers for second hand tins, spoken to representatives from the flour mills. With the reps I knew well, I also discussed the money side. They stated 500 loaves was not enough on their own to make the bakery a success. More discussions with Rosalyn and we decided that if we succeed and grow the bread tally, we will be married in eighteen months. In that time, I would also have to build a one-bedroom home behind the bakehouse.

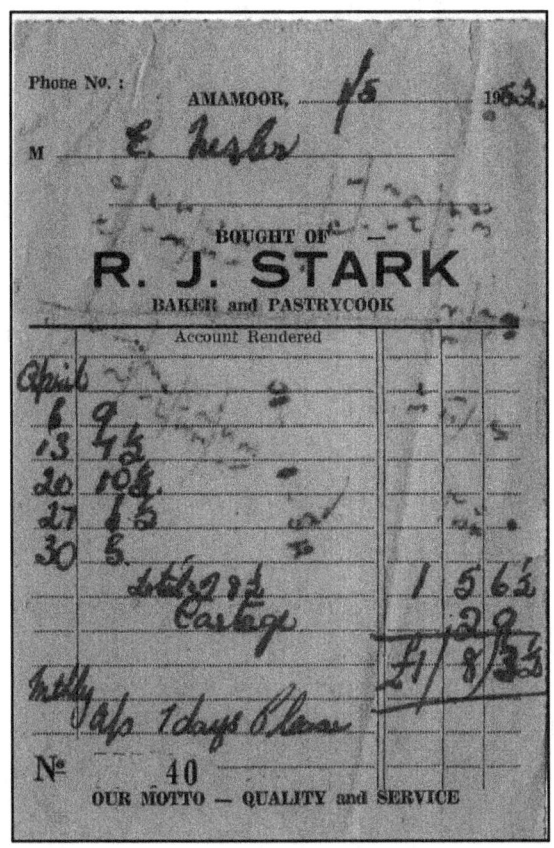
E Nesler's account with Amamoor Bakery 1/5/1952

I would have to 'do up' the sparse, single man's accommodation attached to the bakehouse for me to live in for the time being. (I lived in it for two years). Our wedding day would be away into the future.

I then had another meeting with my cousins, and we drew up a loose 'lease agreement', not registered, that I could do anything I wished with the property. We didn't have plans for our future home, only my rough hand drawings that Rosalyn and I had designed.

Not a word was ever relayed to the general public, but James Fardoolie came to me one afternoon and asked if there was any truth to the rumour that I had bought the bakehouse at Amamoor.

Someone, somewhere, had let the cat out of the bag, as they say. I had to admit to him that it was my intention to re-open Amamoor. I officially released the news to the general public after telling James.

My request for second hand tins, of all descriptions, had borne fruit. A phone call to my father's home a few nights later was from Eric Trisize, the baker in Maryborough. He told me that the Silver Spray Flour Manager, Mr Buckberry, had contacted him asking, "Did he still have those tins that he previously told him he had for sale?" and that "a baker in Amamoor was seeking a wide range of tins". Eric told him that he still had a good supply in hand and that I could come and pick out all that I needed. So, the following Saturday night I caught the Bundaberg Mail Train to Maryborough arriving at 1am Sunday morning. Eric's bakery was only a few blocks from the station. The tins were near new and in good condition. I had a list of what I required, and we struck a deal in cash that was good for both of us. I returned to Gympie on the Rocky Mail Train arriving in Gympie at 1am Monday morning and ready to start work at James's bakery at 5am. Eric packed the tins up, tied the parcels with twine and delivered it to the Maryborough railway station. I received them in excellent condition at Amamoor a few days later.

Those days everything came and went by Steam Train Cargo. Flour, yeast, sugar, and salt, the ingredients for the making of the bread would be the last items for me to order. So far, my money was able to pay for what I bought.

We hadn't set an 'official' opening date and I couldn't give James Fardoolie a finishing date. I still had a full list of things that I had to do and very little money. God was steering all my movements.

I had to shift the Shop from the footpath and join it back onto the bakehouse.

I had to order two new tanks from Stolbergs, the plumbers in Gympie. First though, I had to have the electrical wiring completed both in the bakery and accommodation and apply for electricity to be attached to the property.

Bill stated he would find Stan Ferguson, the Boer War veteran somewhere to move into and bought him a tent and erected it behind the General Store. Stan's pride and joy was the barber's chair that we gave him from out of the shop.

I had also noticed on my earlier visits that there was another gentleman living in a tent on the area that was going to be my wood heap. He worked at the 'thinnings' sawmill in Amamoor. It was owned by Heine and Son of Maryborough.

Bill said. "Leave this to me". He had his sons cut into the creek bank on the other side of the bakery fence and they moved this gentleman and his tent to its new site.

He never bought a loaf of bread from me. He always bought it from the other grocery store in Amamoor that still sold Bill Bullock's bread. He never spoke to me at all, he must have really disliked what Bill and I did in moving him.

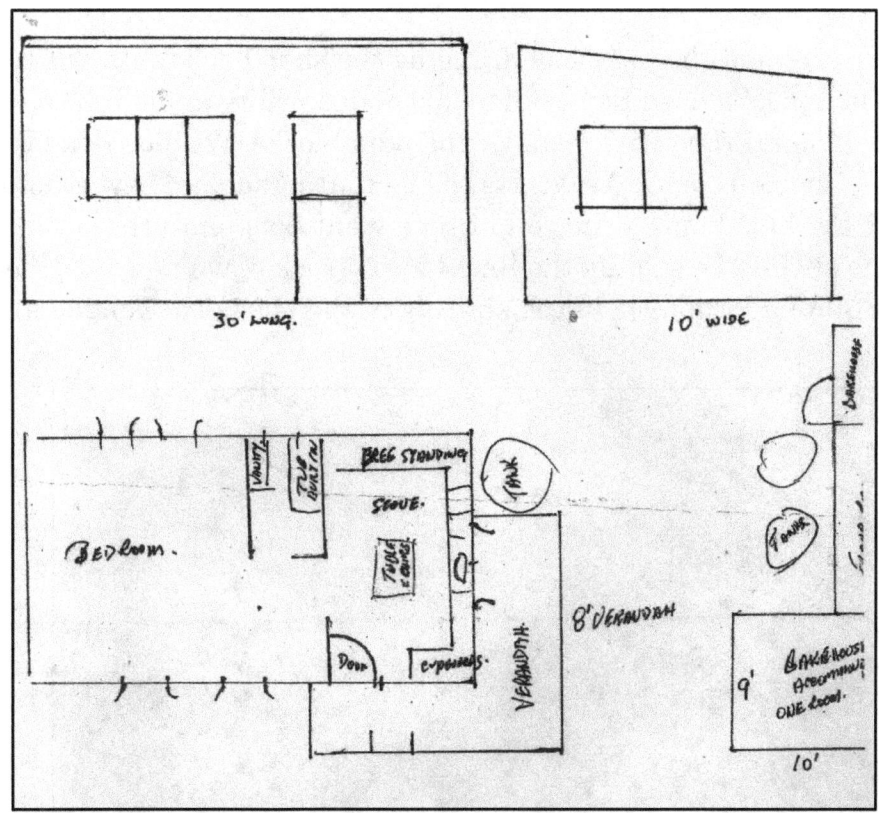

Rough plans for our home at Amamoor

Well, the big clean out day began. First, my accommodation, what a mess! no power as yet. Rosalyn had given me her wood copper and stand from her 'glory box'.

Plenty of hot water had to be on hand for the clean-up. For the time being, we set it up at the back of the General Store and carried the hot water in kerosene tins to the bakehouse. The new tanks had been ordered but hadn't yet arrived. The repaired tank stands were ready for them.

Rosalyn even had the first Hoover Washing Machine in her glory box. She was done with having to wash her timber contractor dad's sap laden clothes by hand.

I had now ordered the first load of hardwood from Sterling's Sawmill at Kandanga.

I built a bathroom outside the accommodation. Goodness knows where Stan had previously washed.

We still had the big job of dragging the shop back to its original position. We used Pop Mullers old dodge utility and a full roll of 1" (25mm) rope with pulleys and stop blocks. We slowly moved the shop off its blocks, across the footpath and onto new stumps at the bakehouse. The roll of rope went back onto the hook in the shop to be sold by the lineal foot. I reckon we had stretched it quite a lot longer in the shifting of the shop. The tongue and

Shop back in front of Amamoor bakehouse

groove timber of the shop was in beautiful condition, so when all was cleaned, boy! it looked a picture.

Bakery & Shop from the front.

On my next visit to Amamoor, I filled the fire box with timber that I had collected from around the property. This was different to the cord wood I was using in Fardoolies' bakehouse in Gympie; but it worked wonderfully. I lit the first fire and everyone from the grocery shop and the Railway Ganger and Fettlers across the road cheered as the smoke went up the chimney. It was all falling into place; we watched the first smoke wend its way into the sky. The next day, the two tanks arrived, and luckily, we did not have long to wait for rain. The tanks were full after a few storms. I ordered all the stock I was going to need, and the supply companies all gave me 30 days credit. I had to have everything in place before I gave James a fortnight's notice.

It was now the 1st of August 1949. Six months had come and gone. I gave Bill my bakery starting date of the 30th August, which allowed me time to give and work out my notice with James Fardoolie and for Bill to cancel his bread order from Bill Bullock. I moved into the single accommodation on Monday 14th August.

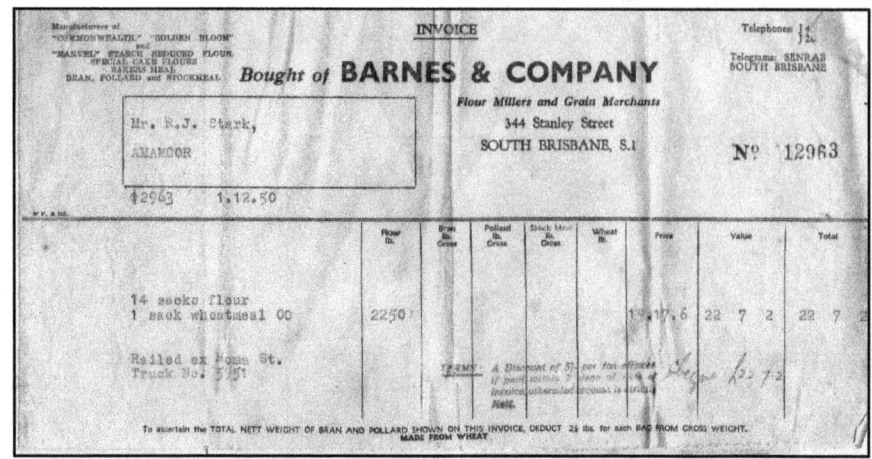

Flour Mill Account and a Receipt

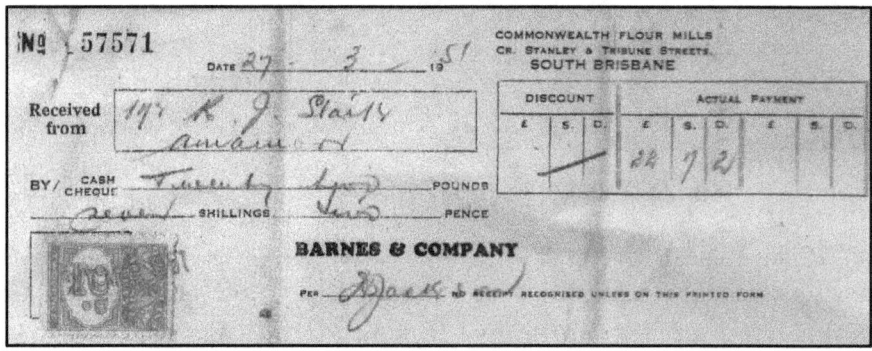

Cliff Harry caught up with me and wished me all the best. He told me that if I was successful, local farmers would be soon buying their bread from me. He said he would probably lose a few customers, along with W & J Condie and James Fardoolie.

The first week it rained cats and dogs. We had set the date for a trial batch of 100 loaves of white bread for Saturday 10th October 1949. I had been firing the oven a few times to gauge the heat from green wood.

All the cooking ingredients, the weighing machine, the galvanized 10-gallon buckets, knives, and scrapers had arrived. Rolls of white paper to wrap the bread in, had arrived from the Courier Mail in Brisbane. White and brown paper bags in small, medium, and large, along with two shipments of Cyco Yeast from Mauri Bros and Thompson in Brisbane. These hessian and calico bags each holding 10 pounds of yeast, came by railway once a week and had to be kept under refrigeration at all times. For the time being, we found a corner in Bill's grocery refrigerator.

Things were now falling into place, I had the Gormley Brothers pineapple carriers call in to my parent's home at 4 Thomas Street, Gympie and pick up my things, mainly my bed and the many wooden boxes holding the things I had collected since my youth. My room at Amamoor was full with a table, wardrobe, my new A.T.C. radio, a new electric immerser to boil my jug and a mentholated fire ring for me to cook my meals on. Living and doing things were hard in those days, but you may smile today, because we thought we were well off.

I told Rosalyn that on the Saturday morning of the trial run, I would be coming to Gympie on the Railmotor to deliver the first cob loaf to her at her shop.

After we were married, Rosalyn and I always had the first cob loaf for our breakfast.

That Friday we were all excited, the town people dropping in and wishing me all the best as I donned my white apron and cap. I loaded the fire box with wood, so that it was ready to light at 5am. All my cousins (except Marie, who ran the exchange till 10 pm and could not leave) were there to watch, plus a few of the locals.

It was something to be involved with this new baker making his first hand-made dough at Amamoor. Silence was in order and the only light was from a few candles and a kerosene lantern at one end of the bakery and a kerosene lamp at the other. Helen had given me this lamp as a good luck gift. It was one of her mother's (my grandfather's sister) clear table lamps. I still have this lamp at the ready in my unit at Palmwoods, 73 years later.

They watched me weigh out all the ingredients that had to go into this first dough and they watched as my skilful hands turned over the flour into the water. Some stayed just for a short while. It took me 5 minutes under 2 hours to completely bind all in place. As I patted the finished dough in its section of the trough, I asked God to bless my work, then a light sprinkle of flour and covered it with clean flour bags. In eight hours, it would have filled that portion of the trough that I had allotted it.

I set my alarm and crawled into my three-quarter sized stretcher, that I had slept on since I was seven years old on the open verandah at Thomas Street. Mother and Dad also gave me the bed sheets and pillows to start me off.

If my venture was successful, I had planned to sleep in this room until I had built our home and Rosalyn and I were married, when I would carry my bride across the threshold into our new home. A beautiful dream!

My alarm went off at 4.30am. I dressed and went in to light the oven fire. It sparkled into life. I then knocked down my dough, that is, I pushed out all the rising. The dough felt great, I left it for another 20 minutes to recover while I laid out my flour bags on the window bench.

My tins were all greased with fat from Herbert's Butcher Shop, six doors up the street. I noticed he had already started his Saturday work too; his electric light was on. I lit my kero lights and started to cut and remove the dough from the trough. I put a section onto the window table where I weighed my dough into 2¼lb (1.02kg) pieces, then with one in each hand I moulded and stacked them in line on the middle work bench (the trough with its lid on) and covered them with bags as I progressed along the bench. I had 106 loaves of bread and two cob loaves.

My dough felt just right. The oven temperature was coming up, just as I hoped and planned. I then started on the first moulded piece of dough. I split it in two equal parts moulded them again and put the loaf shaped dough into the tin ready for its last proving. It did not take me long to complete the tinning of this dough. The uncooked bread was now in their tins under a bag cover, proving for about 30 to 40 minutes. I now made a cuppa in my fireplace and tested the oven for heat, and it was nearly spot on. I lit my dripping slush lamp to use for seeing into the oven. At 6am, I removed the bag covering and double checked all was ready. It was! ... and wonderful to see!

Time was 6.15am. I opened the oven door for a final check of the heat, if it was too hot, I would have swabbed the floor down with water, but it was ready. I took down my peel and placed the 106 loaves into the oven and my two cobs on the bricks. I then closed the door and waited for the 30 minutes cooking time to pass. The aroma was delightful and when I opened the damper of the oven to let off the excess steam you could smell fresh bread all over Amamoor.

Bill, Helen, and family were my first customers. Compared to my opposition, my bread was prize quality, they just could not match this bread. The normal bread the locals were used to would be 24 loaves to a tea chest, my bread was 12 loaves to a tea chest. I just could not calm my excitement, I broke one loaf in half, and the bread threads were like silk. For the people of Amamoor, that day the bread was FREE.

I transferred the full batch to Bill's Grocery Store, except for four loaves, two for each of our parents, one cob for Rosalyn, I ate the other one for my breakfast. I closed up, having the bakehouse all ready for Sunday afternoon when I returned to make the doughs for Monday 12th of October, 1949. The cousins could not believe the size of the bread, and the favourable remarks from the customers; they could not find a fault. The free bread had also helped to win the day.

When I arrived in Gympie on the 9am Rail Motor, I went directly to Rosalyn's shop at the five ways. Friends had already told her the results of my trial baking, but when she saw the bread and the cob loaf, she cried.

Cliff Harry called round to my parent's home that afternoon and arranged to drive me back on Sunday.

Arriving back in Amamoor, he stayed until I had finished my first marketable dough. He sat on the window bench, curled up his legs and watched and talked to me for the two hours it took to make enough dough to produce 175 white and 20 wheatmeal loaves.

I am sure he was proud of me. His father, Mr Reg, along with Cliff and Ted had taught me my trade. By my third week I was making 1600 loaves and growing. Arnolds General Store in Kandanga came to see me and asked me to supply my bread to them. I did feel sad for Billy Bullock because he also lost Mr. Cullen from the Dagun store. The other corner store in Amamoor never came over to me and only sold a few loaves of bread a day.

Advertising Calendar 1952

My bread had lasting quality too. Farmers who went on two weeks holidays, came home, and toasted the bread that had been left in the bread box. No mould! the mixture and the cooking were the answer.

I had already employed Miss Saul of Busby Street to man my shop, but she was not happy. She really wanted to finish her Junior at Gympie State High School.

L-R: Henry & Silvia Dimmick, Rosalyn & John Stark
Photo November, 2005

One of my early customers on horseback was Whistling Wid Collins. You could hear him coming and going. I told him of my shop girl problem, and he said his daughter Sylvia, aged 14 years would love to come and work for me. She started the next day, and we were friends with Sylvia and her husband Henry Dimmick for some 71 years. We stayed close friends with Sylvia's parents till they both passed away. Henry and I lost our life partners 6 and 4 years ago. Henry passed away in 2020.

The Army had at long last contacted me with a discharge date, the 20th January 1950. I was a fully trained soldier in live ammunition, 303 Rifle, Bren Gun, Owen Machine Gun, and The Piet Armor piercing weapons.

In 1952 the Army wrote to me and asked me to re-join as a fully trained infantry personal in the third division to go to Korea. I wrote back stating that I had a one-man business and was married with a young daughter. I thanked them for the offer but declined.

The bakery was making money. No one left town from the forestry. Merv Cooper made sure that the workers paid their bills at the Grocer, Butcher, and Baker before they left town. The only way out of town was by The Mary Valley Rattler Rail Motor. In four years, I only forgot to add 11/- ($1.10) to one of my customers' bills, so it was a wonderful business.

I could start building Rosalyn's and my future home, I ordered the stumps, hardwood timber for the frame, the weatherboards, tongue-and-groove flooring from Sterling's Sawmills at Kandanga. The masonite lining, kitchen cabinets, table and chairs, casement windows and front door I ordered from Collins Joinery Works at Amamoor. The iron roofing was from Cullinane's at Gympie.

Our finished home at Amamoor - 1950

At long last, Rosalyn and I set our Wedding Day for the 20th January 1951, at the Surface Hill Methodist Church where both of us grew up and all the waiting, longing and writing came to an end.

Gympie's main street came to a stop at 7.15pm as we came out of Murrays Studios after having our wedding photos taken. With the Scottish Pipe Band playing in the background, all we could see was a sea of faces. They did not come to see me! but wanted to see what Gympie's main seamstress had designed for herself and her bridesmaids.

L-R: Merv Patterson, June Pritchard, John Stark, Rosalyn Stark (nee Pritchard), Ron Pritchard, Elizabeth (Beth) Stark.

The Surface Hill Ladies Guild did the catering for our wedding breakfast attended by our mums and dad's relations and friends. While speeches and toasts were happening, my mates had jacked up the borrowed Morris Z ute and tied boots, shoes, and lots of tins, setting us up for a good send off. They chased us out of town. We stopped at the end of the tar road at Monkland and removed all the rattle and noise from our back bumper (like many before and after us) and set off for Surfers Paradise on the dirt road in the photo.

We had engaged Mr Eric Pailthorpe from Daigun and Mike Slaughter from Amamoor to be his offsider, to make the doughs and bake the bread while we were away. They lived locally, although I had never met Eric. I thought he may have wanted to meet me to find out my routine, but no, he kept his distance. Mike moved into the single accommodation attached to the bakehouse.

Sylvia was now running the shop helped, if necessary, by cousin Bill.

End of bitumen at Monkland, heading south to Brisbane

We returned from a wonderful week at Surfers. It would take another book to tell this beautiful story, but we had to come back to earth, this story was for Rosalyn and I to live, for our 67½ happy years.

*Rosalyn and I enjoyed each other's company and we loved each other fully. We never had a harsh word to each other. While Ros was in Brisbane for six weeks sewing, getting the dresses ready for our youngest daughter Jenny's wedding, I decided to grow a moustache.

When Ros stepped out of her car, she took one look at me and stated, "I'm not kissing that thing!" I never grumbled. "That Thing" came off before tea.

Short lived moustache

When she was called home to heaven, on the 15.10.2017, she left me with four wonderful children, whom we love beyond compare. As this book is written we have 12 grandchildren, 24 great grandchildren, 4 great, great grandchildren and another 2 on the way. What a wonderful story to leave this world*.

We arrived home in Gympie on Saturday evening, and we stayed at Mum and Dad Pritchard's home in Iron Street. On Sunday morning we loaded all our furniture and belongings onto the tray back on Dad Pritchard's truck. Our bedroom suite was built by Prongers Joinery of Monkland Street.

Amamoor had welcomed us home with open arms. Sunday night was back to making doughs, these had increased to two doughs a night. An eight hour and a six-hour dough. Up to now, what with building our home and dough making, cooking, delivering to three stores and the forestry, I was not having too many hours sleep.

With Rosalyn now looking after me, we decided to make pies and pasties for locals and the forestry workers. Our trade just advanced in leaps and bounds.

The town set Saturday week in the Amamoor Hall to 'tin kettle' (bring presents and have a party) our return. The weekend came but it was pouring rain from a cyclone off the coast. I had ordered an 18gallon (64litres) keg of beer and it had been delivered from the hotel at Kandanga for the function that night. All was prepared, but with the cyclone hitting the coast, we thought it was cancelled. I didn't count on the men of Amamoor turning up at the Hall and carrying on without us. I was told they were all blind drunk in the grass gutter outside the hall in the pouring rain at 11 pm. We could not see the other side of the railway line beside us, let alone get up to the Hall in that blinding rain.

They told us all about it after the flood went down, but the town didn't put on another party for us. I do not know if any presents were given. They probably took them back home with them, that is, if they were in any condition to remember them.

1929 Chev

I bought a 1929 Chevrolet utility. I used this ute to carry my flour from the rail goods shed, six bags at a time, plus salt, sultanas, and general merchandise. This carrying only lasted a few months before I engaged Gormley's to pick up and deliver all my goods at the railway goods shed.

In late 1951, my alarm went off and I tried to sit up in bed, to find both my arms were asleep, as dead as door nails. I woke Rosalyn and with her help managed to dress and walk over to the bakehouse to knock down the first dough. By the time I had finished knocking the dough down, the feeling had started to come back into both my arms. We thought that I must have slept on my arms cutting the blood flow off from my hands. Over the next few weeks, it kept happening on and off. I was starting to not want to go to bed. We booked an appointment with Dr

Outridge in Gympie. He in turn made an appointment with a specialist on Wickham Terrace in Brisbane.

I ordered a brand-new Singer Utility from Doug Burton and had to wait six months for delivery. I traded my 1929 Chev in as deposit.

I never put in for the phone service to be connected to the bakery. The couple of phone calls I made each year did not warrant the expense of a telephone. Where would we be today in this situation?

I rang my dad from the Post Office and asked him if he would like to come to Brisbane with me for company. He said he would love to. I made arrangements to pick him up at his home at 4:30am next Wednesday. My appointment was for 1.30pm.

Rosalyn holding Lynette aged 7 weeks

With Lynette only a month old, Rosalyn decided to stay and keep the home fires burning, just as well as things turned out.

On Tuesday I started work at 10am, to make the bread for Wednesday. I explained what was going on to the Arnold's and asked if they would come down on Wednesday to pick up their bread and they were only too happy.

Cullens bread always went on the Rail Motor. Rosalyn and Bill would see to that. The forestry was a different kettle of fish, so I decided to deliver all their bread after tea that night.

I was delivering my last round close to 9pm, when I ran across Mr and Mrs Luther's front lawn. In the dark, not seeing the garden tap, I tripped over it, hurting my left leg. I gave it a good rub, finished my deliveries, and headed for home and a bath.

Rosalyn looked at my leg, it was puffed up and looking sore, so she placed hot packs on it, and I went off to bed. I woke when the alarms went off at 3:45am (you know, Lynette never woke to any of the alarms going off, which was great). I had a quick cuppa with Ros and with my leg still feeling very sore, limped off to the car, I picked up dad and headed off for the four-and-a-half-hour drive to Chermside, an outer suburb of Brisbane.

We stopped half-way down the highway at the Log Cabin Café for a cup of tea, it was in the middle of the trip, on the left side of the road at the Caloundra turnoff. Dad asked if I was alright to drive. My leg was so tight in my trousers, I couldn't feel it, so I kept driving. We arrived at the doctors early and Dad explained my plight to the nurse.

Dr Cooner said he would see me now. I came to see him about my arms, and I quickly explained to him my trouble with them.

He then looked at my leg, he said, "oh my gosh" and quickly positioned me on his examining table. He took a pair of scissors and cut up my good strides from the hem to the hip and he asked me how it had happened. I told him and he said that unfortunately I had broken one of my main arteries in the thigh. I had an enormous blood clot and hospital was the next urgent move. The phone rang hot to Rosalyn and Dad was on his way home.

Rosalyn rang Cliff and Ted Harry and explained what had happened to me. They were so good, they straight away said they would supply all the bread for us.

Dad, not knowing that Rosalyn had the bakery all in hand, was phoning around Gympie trying to buy a small amount of bread from each the bakeries. Rosalyn sent him packing. Dad always referred to Rosalyn as "John's Pepper Pot."

The first week the Harry Brothers delivered the next day's bread late at night. With Lyn only weeks old and Rosalyn only just starting to learn to drive the Singer. This is where my mate Selwyn Dellit came to the fore. After the first week, Rosalyn and Selwyn would drive the Singer into town and collect the hot bread from Harry's after 10:30pm.

In the meantime, I was placed in a deep sleep for 23 hours a day, under the watchful eye of the Sister-In-Charge. I was always woken around 3pm each day. I can still see the Sister giving me the red substance. The effect was near instant. She would fade away from my sight.

Three weeks had gone by, and Rosalyn asked Selwyn drive her and Lyn to Brisbane to see me. From then on Rosalyn would come to Brisbane by train. The hospital arranged accommodation with a Mrs Millicent who lived close by. Rosalyn would leave Lyn with her and slip over to the hospital and sit holding my hand, in between feed times.

While all this was going on, I was also being treated for the damaged nerve in my spine. Dr Cooner told me that he looked into the Australian Medical Records and there was only one other case recorded, a baker in South Australia. With rest, the damaged nerve was slowly recovering, and I would soon be back at work. By keeping me asleep and my leg still, the hospital was slowly winning in dissolving the clot. My leg was all the colours of the rainbow. But I was not out of the woods yet, I had quite a time getting back to full strength. Rosalyn, my family, and friends kept up their prayers for my recovery.

Home again after 16 weeks in hospital, it was lovely turning my first dough. The customers were thrilled to have me back again and the Luther family were extra happy that I had survived the blood clot.

Four months after I had re-opened Amamoor Bakery, I had a sales rep call in and sell me a membership with MBF (Medical Benefits Fund) for 5/- a month. After my release from hospital, I received a nice cheque from them.

With all the extra bread load, I finally gave thought to investing in a dough making machine. I asked around for information on any available second-hand machines. The big drag on our income with me being off work for so long, I was always looking to save pennies.

A few weeks later I received a letter from a Real Estate in Brisbane, telling me he was selling equipment from the Spring Hill Bakery, which was being taken over by Tip Top Bread of Nundah, a couple of suburbs away. For £50 ($100) I could buy the complete dough machine. It was made by Brown and Kidd. An open U shape. I made arrangements to come down the following Thursday (our lightest day of baking for the week). The machine was in reasonable condition and a reasonable price. The real estate said he would deliver the machine to Amamoor by railway freight and that he would pay the cost.

About a week later a customer came into the bakehouse and stated someone in town was buying a cement mixer and it had arrived by the goods train during the night. I never said a word, I phoned the Gormley boys and asked them to deliver it to the bakehouse. Well, what a surprise when it arrived. I not only received the dough machine; I think they also got rid of half the machinery in the bakery.

The whole bakery in Spring Hill was belt driven. From the motor, all the 2" (5.08cm) drive rods, leather belting and cup links, the huge wooden wheels that gave the slow down gearing for the dough machine, I got the lot! I could not fit this all into my little bakery!

I rang up my sister Joyce's husband Irv Runge who was a mining engineer working with his two brothers taking the gold tailings out of the sand along the banks of the Mary River. They brought the sand to the treatment plant near Albert Park and put it into 12' (3.65m) vats and then treated the sand with Cyanide which settled the gold to the bottom. They also had the Tamaree Lime Works. Joyce and Irv came out after tea and viewed all that we had received. Irv took pen and paper and drew up a plan to reduce the size of the machine to fit into my bakehouse.

I had to have three phase power connected as I needed a 10-horse powered electric motor to drive the mixing bowl.

Irv removed a seven-ton gear box from one of the Australian Army Bren Gun Carriers, one of many they had bought from the army after the war. They were all in storage next door in the old office yard of the mine called "The Scottish of Monkland". Irv took all the rods and steel back to the family workshop and welded together a frame to carry the motor and the gear box. It was all driven by four V belts 3' (91cm) long. I mixed the dough perfectly in first gear and used reverse to tip the bowl on its side and all I had to do was guide the dough into the trough. It was wonderful and it looked so grand. I could hardly wait to finally move the dough machine into the bakery.

1st Hiccup! The door to the bakery was only 3' (91cm) wide, the machine bowl was 5' (1.52m) wide so I removed the door and widened the entrance to double its width giving me a 6' (1.83m) doorway.

2nd Hiccup! I had to reduce the size of the table on the flour room wall to accommodate the dough machine's two legs that held the big bowl. All went well with the help of Selwyn and Mike Slaughter.

Mike was a customer who later on came to work for us and live in the accommodation room.

3rd Hiccup! To solve the problem of how to lift this big mixing bowl into the bakery and onto its stand. The three of us, plus the cousins next door, could only lift the bowl a little off the floor.

Ros came over and said, "we are in luck!" The Gympie City Electric Light truck and six men had just arrived to change the power rating into the bakehouse, so Rosalyn went over to them on the footpath and nicely asked them to help out.

You could not move in the bakehouse! we could not get enough men on three sides to lift together. Plenty of suggestions, but none worked well enough to do the job. We had advanced enough to have the bowl up on boxes at hip height. But we still had to lift the bowl 6' (1.83m) to clear the yokes (legs). They all left giving me more suggestions on what I could do.

The next move was an endless chain, hooked up to the ceiling. No trouble!

4th Hiccup! You would not believe it, no manhole in the bakehouse, so I had to make one. Would you believe it, no rafter above the bowl, so I would have to place a piece of solid hardwood 6" (15.2cm) x 4" (10cm) x 6' (1.82m)in the ceiling to carry the weight of the bowl. I shot up to Merv Collins at the joinery and came back with a piece 7' (2.13m) long, so I had to enlarge the manhole to be able to locate the timber right over the bowl and then cut another hole into the ceiling to accommodate the endless chain, which I borrowed from Claude Griffiths of Amamoor Motors. Within twenty minutes the bowl was in the leg stands.

The Electrician had been out and the power to the motor had already been connected through a switching gear, to accommodate the load.

Irv arrived after he finished work at 4pm and bolted all his steel work into place. After I had cleaned down all the new equipment, Irv stayed to witness the making of the first dough.

I poured the water I needed into the bowl for the dough. In the past, I always lifted the bags of flour I would need onto the table for easier pouring. So, I placed the flour bags on the table as usual and opened the tops, I then poured the flour sideways into the bowl, then swung to bowl into the upright position, put in the lock and started the motor. If we did not lock the bowl in place, the first revolution would dump the contents onto the floor .... I have been in other bakeries where their dough man has placed many a dough on the floor.

I was very anxious to see if this new machine would make the doughs equal to my hand-made ones. I was not disappointed with the results, and it only took 15minutes to make the first dough. We were all so pleased!

When Chubba Dan, the cream carrier, backed into the bakery the next day to load bread direct into the cream cans, he noticed the high bread fitted tight as usual. The talk of the town was that machine made doughs would make a tighter dough and so would not rise as much ... we put them all to shame.

Rosalyn and I bought a Commander refrigerator from Fred Cox to store our yeast in, as well as all our perishable goods. In summer, I used to have blocks of ice transported out in large bags of sawdust on the 3:30pm rail motor from the Butter Factory in Gympie. The ice helped to cool the water down and allow for proper fermentation of the doughs.

In the early days to get cold water, all bakeries had wells, underground cement tanks, or bores with windmills attached. I only had above ground tanks, so I had to use ice to cool the water down for use in my bakery.

The 4th birthday of the bakery was coming up. My shoulders weren't in a good condition. Lyn was nearly one year old when we made the decision to sell. We placed a price based on production of loaves and put an advert in the Baker's Journal. We sold within a week to Mr. Sid Pennell Snr. of Laidley.

We moved out and stored our furniture in my parent's neighbour's garage, our refrigerator went into my mother's kitchen. She had never had a fridge before. Ice was usually delivered by Mr Blake three times a week. My young brother Len thrived on ice cream. Home refrigerators were a very new thing.

Bakers Journal – July Cover 1951

Sid Pennell had his own utility. His boys now ran the Laidley bakery, Amamoor was his baby. Sylvia and Mike now had a full-time job trying to save the business. Syd would go home to Laidley on Saturday and come back Tuesday. I'm afraid he only lasted just under 12 months and sold out to two brothers.

They in turn, bought the deeds of the bakery property from Mrs Gardener who now owned the Grocery Store. The boys extended the bread deliveries to Imbil, Kandanga, Tuchekoi, and Brooloo.

After a while they replaced the dough machine with a smaller Brown and Kidd One Arm, only taking up half the space of the old one.

The Kandanga and Imbil bakeries closed down. The onslaught of supermarkets and hot bread shops soon put an end to this type of bakery and deliveries to the home. The brothers closed the Amamoor Bakery in 1969.

The property was sold to a pottery firm who updated the heat structure of the oven to high degrees. The dough machine was now making and mixing clay.

Rosalyn and I called in to see them and they showed us around and how they were altering our home. They had extended the house making it into a three-bedroom home and added an extension on the bakehouse. The day we called in to see them, the carpenters were pulling out our bathtub and refitting it into the new bathroom. Our kitchen, dining and bathroom areas were now a large lounge room.

By the photo you can see the removal of the bakehouse. The oven stood out in the weather for many years. I was told it was removed brick by brick and reassembled in Pomona at a Pizza Shop. My dough trough ended in a farmer's paddock as a feed trough.

The late photos show the difference ... only memories now!

Amamoor - Rosalyn & Lynette in front of the remains of the oven. Photo 1995

Amamoor is now only a shell of its former self! The General Store had an extension added on the side, catering for take-away meals. The second Grocery Store is now a family home. The National Bank has been removed and replaced by a new home. Herbert's Butcher Shop is a Coffee Shop and Take Away. The Heine's Sawmill and loop railway into the sawmill is gone.

Someone in Amamoor tried to tell me that the sawmill was on the left side of the railway line. No! it was where the aeroclub is now located. The C.O.D. (Fruit Marketing Board) and its hardware shop is now bare ground. The Railway Gangers and the Fettlers sheds are gone and the little bridge below the bakehouse is now a pipe under the road to the new bridge over Amamoor Creek.

A park with tables for the public is now on the bank of Amamoor Creek. The State School was moved into town from the corner of Dagun and Amamoor Creek Roads.

All gone are the forestry's houses and camps. No1 married quarters, then a camp area, is now a park. The main married and single barracks camp area further up the creek are gone, replaced with now 50' (15.24m) high pine trees.

Memories! ... I wonder where those hundreds of men, women and children are now? Do they ever think of the young baker who took his dream and turned it into reality?

Chapter 19

Harry Bros, incorporating W & J Condie
32 – 38 Reef Street, Gympie
1952-1970

In 1952, at the old bakery in Duke Street, big discussions were happening in reference to the viability of repairing the bakery. The clay mortar in the brick building was in very poor condition and falling away, needing many repairs.

Tom Bradley had left to join the State Public Service, leaving a very real problem of nobody wanting the job handling horse and carts. After many, many years of faithful service, Col the Horse was also ready to be retired to the Long Paddock to spend his last years grazing.

I remember before Tom Bradley came to work for Harry's they went through about six carters over a three-year period, it was getting hard then to find staff who could properly handle horses.

The Harry's decided to approach Henry Condie, the last of the brothers to still be involved with the bakehouse that their Grandfather James built in Reef Street. The Condie's were still the greatest producers of bread in Gympie with nine carters doing all the deliveries to Hospitals, Shops, Motels, Hotels and door to door. Tom Condie and Fardoolie's were the only other bakeries to still have horse and cart deliveries.

Cliff Harry made an offer to Henry to take over W & J Condie and it was accepted. Henry would not stay and work for Harry Brothers. I understand Religion had something to do with the decision. On completion of the sale, he went to work for his brother Thomas at the Stewart Terrace Bakery.

Steve Heilbronn was wanting to retire. His 1938 Morris van was falling to pieces, and he felt it was time to sit back and enjoy his remaining years. Steve had worked in the Duke Street bakery all his life. Firstly for Longs, then Bill Blakeway, followed by Reg Harry, and lastly the Harry Brothers. I am sure he would be remembered by all who knew him as a kind and happy person.

Harrys bought their staff across from Duke Street, only requiring the two dough makers and the nine carters to remain. Gratten Emerson was completing his trade as Baker Pastry Cook.

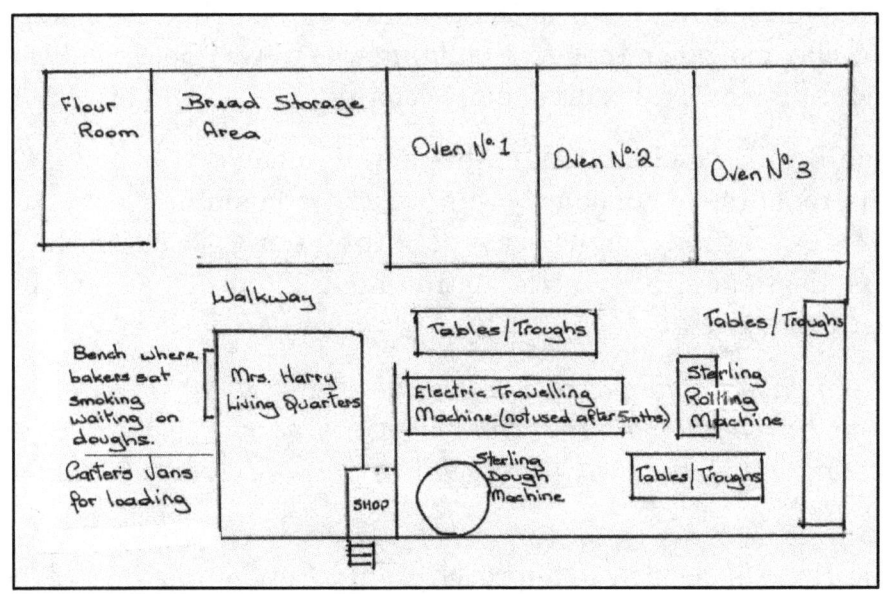

Mud map of Harry Bros. inc. W & J Condie

In the 10 months of 1954-1955 I was working with them again as a Master Baker, no cakes or pastries were produced. Doug Roy and I were flat out on №3 oven baking bread. Doug's nephew, Les McGuiness, was working №1 oven with Ray Paywell as jobber. Cliff Harry was on №2 oven with Ted Harry as jobber and on oven n°3 was Doug Roy with me as jobber.

It had been many years since Doug and I had worked together. Doug stayed all his working years with the Harry Family.

When I returned, that large electric steel travelling oven was still in place, it was a real problem working around this machine.

I do not know what happened to that oven. I never thought to ask my mate, Doug Roy.

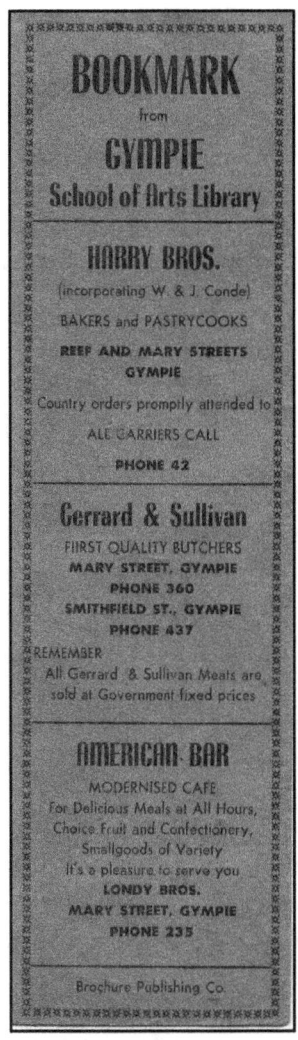

Cliff was still expanding as the bread tally in Gympie from the local Bakeries was steadily falling. The carter's section was always busy. No horses anymore. Panel vans now doing all the workload. It was bedlam all day long, so many men and women trying to load their bread and buns. Cliff Harry certainly became the largest Bakery that Gympie ever knew.

I am afraid that Ted's liking of strong drink plus all the business worries added stress to their marriage and Joyce divorced Ted, took their two boys, and moved back to live with her parents at Roma on the Darling Downs.

As the trade was shrinking rather greatly now, the family once again came together to discuss the future of their family business.

In 1959, Ted walked out of the Harry Brothers partnership bankrupt and penniless and Mrs Reg Harry (Kath) came back into the business to help Cliff. The business name was not changed.

In 1955, I purchased a two-year lease of the Forest Hill Bakery and in 1956, Gratten came and worked for me for a few months.

*After the Forrest Hill lease finished, I went to work at the Nudgee Bakery for three years as $^{No}2$ oven man and while I was there, Ted Harry came in one night to work as my Jobber and filled me in with all the news from Gympie. It was sad! I had a very soft spot for Ted, he was more like a brother. He poured his heart out to me that night as we were working. He had given up drinking.

Envelope from Forest Hill Bakery

He dearly loved and missed Joyce and his boys, so he walked away from Gympie taking nothing with him and was starting a new life. He was making his way to Roma, hoping that Joyce would forgive him and take him back*.

Kathleen (Kath, as she was known), was a lovely woman. Working with Cliff, they both tried hard to hold the business together, the supermarkets would not allow any of Gympie's Bakeries to supply bread to their stores.

Brisbane's two big bakeries had it all tied up, no one could match the discounts that being big can give.

*I found that out when working as Night Manager at the new Woolworths store in Stanthorpe. I personally took on one of these bread companies ... and won! I can still see six gondolas of Brisbane baked bread and all they allowed this local baker was one gondola of their bread ...

I called into the store in 2017, while travelling through with my son and to my surprise the little bakery was still there after 36 years and still supplying Woolworths with one gondola. They had held on even when the big boys tried hard to shift them. But the owners had the support of local customers. Sometimes she had to refill that gondola three times a day. She said they are not going to beat her. It was lovely to see and talk with her again. This is the determination of country Bakers, trying to hold on under such huge difficulties*.

The Harrys were here to stay as well. They employed Bill Dunmore, an accountant, to sort out which was the best way for them to go. It is true "Life is not meant to be easy", Bill advised them to try and control a big section of bread sales in Gympie and to close the town shop in Mary Street. They took this advice seeing that Hilda Moore was to be married to Les Kidd shortly and they lost their shop girl.

Bill Dunmore also advised Cliff to approach Tom Condie at the Stewart's Terrace Bakery and make an offer to take over the business. Cliff went and saw Tom Condie, the sale contract was signed, the purchase completed, the money exchanged and only the celebration to come.

Cliff and Glen went to bed, they kissed goodnight and at 1am on the 29th January, 1965, Cliff was woken with terrific pains in his chest and before anyone could help, had passed away.

Exactly the same as his father Reg. Both 42 years of age, both with no previous heart problems but both smoked in excess. Those days there weren't any warnings on the dangers of smoking.

Kathleen approached Tom when he came to pay his respects and Kath asked him to rescind the sale, but Tom in the 'Condie way' stated "A sale is a sale". This broke Kathleen's heart and she wished she could change her life.

Mrs Kathleen Harry now had the widest coverage of bread deliveries in Gympie's history. She had 13 carters and trucks. John Colls from "Colls Motor Clinic" told me he had the contract to look after all these vehicles.

She took stock of it all and a long fight began. My friend, Doug Roy, stood by her and advised her in many matters. The staff were wonderful, but trade was still dropping dramatically and eventually Kathleen moved back into the old Duke Street bakery home with Glen and her family. She battled on for a few years, but finally walked away from the Reef Street Bakery and told Bill Dunmore he could have it. He offered her a token amount, then registered the sale and moved into the living quarters.

Glen and Cliff's family grew up and moved away from home. Glen remarried and went to live with her new husband in Cooroy.

Rosalyn and I had not been back to Gympie for some time as Rosalyn's parents were now living at Dingo, where her dad and brother, Ron, were cutting and hauling timber from Blacktown Mountain to Heine and Son Sawmill in Dingo. The maintenance of their Gympie home was left to when they could travel and attend to the lawns and gardens. They would then come through to us in Brisbane for a few days, before they returned to Dingo.

I had bought a Plastics Factory at Stafford and Rosalyn had her Drapery Store at Milton. We were living at Keperra in Brisbane.

18 years had slipped by since I last had anything to do with bread making. We had not contacted Doug and Betty, so we had no knowledge what was happening in Gympie, although I knew of small bakeries going broke in many places.

*In the above Photo in 2019, the roof marked with an X
is all that remains of the large bakery.*

Today, this bakery is no more, the building's now in new hands, but it will always stand as the largest Gympie Bakery in the production of bread and in the hands of the Condie family for 74 years.

All the new buildings are made of brick and have 5 new tenants' and the block on which James Condie had built his home is now an empty block owned by the Freemasons Hotel for customer parking. So sad, so many memories!

I often stand at Cliff's grave and wish that it did not happen. He is buried just over from another friend of mine, Ron Tattnell, who died the same way, though Ron had never smoked. Ron passed away on 31/10/2003 at 69 years of age.

Kathleen was not finished with Gympie. More in chapter 22.

Chapter 20

Allen, Lesley, and Henry Condie-Bakers
42 Pine Street, Gympie.
1952-1956

After Tom and his wife's retirement to 19 Stewart Terrace, his brothers were still living in their parent's home at 11 Mulcahy Terrace and they decided that they were not going to allow the Harrys free reign supplying locally baked bread for Gympie.

Hot bread shops were springing up all over the place, so the three brothers bought the land at 42 Pine Street not far from the Nestlés Factory.

Bakery built by Condie brothers at 42 Pine Street. Photo 2018

They approached Dave English to build a Bakehouse for them. In reality it was really a big Hot Bread Shop. They purchased a steel Gardener Travelling Oven, able to cook 200 loaves an hour and being the only Bakery at this end of town they were hoping to cash in on Nestlés 24hour shift workers of 300 staff heading to and from work.

I'm afraid their dream was short lived. People stayed with their normal suppliers of bread, leaving them to rethink their future. The big boys were waiting on the sidelines and in 1956 they moved in and made the brothers an offer.

They sold before they went broke. The big boys turned this building into a distribution point for all the deliveries in and around Gympie. They put the distribution out to tender and a Gympie man won the contract.

In 1989 the distribution centre was moved to a new building in the industrial estate and the building was again sold and changed into "The Feed Barn", selling feed for all livestock, birds, and country living. This firm is still trading in 2022.

Allen passed away in 1974. Lesley died in 1985. Tom in 1989 and Henry in 1998.

A large extension was added to the Condie residence at Mulcahy Terrace in the 1990s.

11 Mulcahy Terrace - Photo 2020

In the year 2022, there aren't any Condies from the original family living in or around Gympie.

Chapter 21

Bill Dunmore
32-38 Reef Street, Gympie
1970-1972

You have read how the Harrys battled to survive the tragic downturn both in trade and the sad loss of Cliff.

The collapse of Harry Brothers in 1959 when Ted left the partnership and Cliff's death in 1965 left Kathleen Harry along with Doug Roy, Les McGinnis, and Ray Paywell trying hard to hold on to what was left of the Harry business empire until 1970.

Bill Dunmore had taken over the company for a small token cash payment and with a little help from his friends, struggled for the next two years and finally in 1972 he went into liquidation, and all was sold up.

When I finally found Cliff's two daughters in 2017, I arranged to meet Beryl and Janine at Beryl's home on the road to Tin Can Bay. Cliff and Glen's children had grown and married. They told me what little of the family they knew. It felt strange that I could tell them a lot more of the family they knew nothing about.

Trevor and David live in town. Peter married and lives at Moore. I nursed young Reg, their eldest brother, as a baby, but he was not mentioned.

None of Cliff and Glen's children followed their dad into the baking business*

*Their Aunty Elaine became a doctor and married Dr. Ron Waters from Gympie and moved to Perth. They could not tell me of any family living in Perth. Beryl said that over the intervening years they all lost contact with each other.

I told them of our home at 2 Iron Street and the big flood that hit Gympie in 1955, (when I was working for Cliff and Ted in Reef Street for 10 months).

2 Iron St. Flood of 1955
Picture from Rosalyn's parent's home at 7 Iron St.

Doug Roy and I would meet at the old Duke Street Bakery at 4:40am and walk together to Reef Street Bakery.

They knew nothing of Bill Dunmore. They had never met him as children. They might have heard mention of his name in conversations between their parents as Bill Dunmore was their family Accountant, but they weren't sure.

It was a wonderful morning spending four hours catching up with part of Glen and Cliff's family after all those years. I hope that someday I may be able to tell them more*.

I have no knowledge of what happened to Bill Dunmore.

Chapter 22

Mrs Kathleen Harry - Owner - The Brown Jug
79 Mary Street Gympie.
1970-1973

The Brown Jug has been a café for more than 50 years. I remember as a little boy, my Uncle, Clem Degener, (my mother's brother) was a friend of Len Smith the then owner of The Brown Jug Café. The building had been owned by the Patrick family since before I can remember.

In those days, the Brown Jug was only half the size of the present café. Upstairs was Mr. Spear's Accountancy business who employed my eldest sister, Gertrude (Trudy).

The café had at the left door entrance post, a permanent Chewing Gum Machine. Four chews for a penny, opposition to Wrigley's, the company removed it when WW2 broke out in 1939.

Mr Smith was one of the lucky people who could afford a motor car way back in 1936 and would give my uncle a lift home at the end of the day.

Less horses and sulkies were coming into town as more farmers were now buying cars and getting them cut down to utilities. Fords and Chev's were the most common makes in Gympie.

When future owners bought the freehold of the building, they punched through the brick wall between the café and Quaties Shoe Store. The builders put in a steel header and made the café twice the size — to what it is today.

Mrs Harry bought the three-year lease of The Brown Jug Café back in 1970. Kath took the opportunity of adding a Sponge Shop to the café as there wasn't any opposition in Gympie making cakes and pastries. It was a café and milk bar in the evening, catering to customers of the Liberty Picture Theatre across the street.

Kath asked my friend, Doug Roy, who was a whizz with sponges, to join her in the venture.

Doug told me he had a ball working there! Nearly died in summertime, as out the back of the shop was a sheer cliff 40' (12.1m) high of solid blue rock only 4' (1.2m) from the back door. No air flow what-so-ever could make its way into the back of shop.

Doug had two electric ovens, bowls, mixers, trays, and tins, along with the café's gas stove and meal preparation area all jammed into this small space.

There was no air conditioning in those days, only electric fans, so you can imagine how hot the small room was.

The owners of the café have a mural of the waitresses and shop

The Brown Jug Cafe. Photo 2021.

staff of the 1930/40 era, blown up to fill one side wall. It is lovely to see, I personally knew them all.

Kathleen Harry certainly made her profit with this investment move, though she could not have had this success without Doug.

Doug told me he had sponge orders coming out of his ears, so they say, keeping him busy all day. At home, for his own profit, he also squeezed in icing cakes for all occasions.

Kate sure was lucky to have an employee and life-time friends in Doug and Betty Roy. Likewise, Rosalyn and I.

When Kathleen's lease was finished. She sold up all that she still owned in Gympie and moved to Perth to live with her daughter and son in law, Drs. Elaine and Ron Waters.

Doug and Betty lived out their retirement in Gympie. After Rosalyn and I retired back to Gympie in 1983 we continued our close friendship, both couples in the Uniting Church and the forming of the first Gympie Probus Club.

In Probus, we all enjoyed many wonderful trips and celebrations. Doug and I held many positions throughout the years. I was made a Life Member in 2013. The club was 38 years old on the 21st of October 2021.

Rosalyn and I would have liked to have had Kathleen as a closer friend, our paths crossed many times from 1944 to 1956. Being a Salvation Army Captain and a fellow Christian, we could converse so easily. She had a lovely personality.

Looking back, as I can do now, and seeing what Kathleen's life was like, we may have been able to help her a little more and made her life a little easier. Hindsight is perfect, isn't it! If I had said yes to some things, instead of no. I feel sure things would have been better for her.

Betty sadly passed away in 1997, Doug in 2003, Kathleen passed away in Perth in 2004.

All our children played a very important part of our lives during those working years. We all had young families, our darling Lynette played with her brother, Ken, alongside all the young children at the Surface Hill Methodist Sunday School. There are three staff left of Harry's original workers from 1944 to 1965. Hilda Kidd (nee Moore), Colin McBride, and me, John Stark.

My son, Trevor, and I visited The Brown Jug in early October 2021. I was very disappointed to see the mural had disappeared. The present owners had painted the wall white.

Chapter 23

Butcher Shops around Gympie, 1870-2021.

I am not writing especially about Butchers, but I wish to make notice of my friends who were butchers.

Mr Gillamo had one of the earliest Butcher Shops in Gympie and his shop was on the corner of Lawrence Street and Horseshoe Bend. On rainy days, his shop awning was our second stopover on the way home from school. Our first stop was the awning of Marshall's Shop halfway up Lawrence Street on the left (now an Optometrist), before we ran sopping wet to home in Turners Lane, now Thomas Street. Mr. Gillamo supplied Mother with meat in the early days, he had Mr. Stroggins deliver our meat parcel on a beautiful chestnut horse. I can still hear the creak of the leather as Mr. Stroggins leaned over our front fence to give me the parcel of meat. He carried a big basket covered by a white cloth, somehow attached to his left leg.

William Weller Jnr. (he did not stay in the baking profession). He did his trade at Lister's Butcher Shop in Apollonian Vale, opposite Branch's Bakery. After he finished his apprenticeship, he bought the butcher shop from Mr. Lister.

William's shop is still there today, though now it is a Fish and Chip shop. But, if you lift your eyes, the bases for the hanger rails that carried the meat are right around the back wall. In my mind I can still see this layout from 1934.

William Weller Jnr's Butcher Shop - Photo 2018

Mervyn Weller followed his father William jnr. into the butcher trade.

After he finished his apprenticeship, he built a new shop at 169 Brisbane Rd, Monkland. After selling, it became a Bait Shop with a large Alvey reel on the roof. Now it is a Pool Shop.

169 Brisbane Road, Monkland

The next was Gomersalls Butcher in Mary Street.

Archie Drummond - Butcher, opposite the Memorial Gates. This spot is where Condies Arcade is today.

Matt Drummond's Butcher Shop

Matt Drummond, Archie's twin brother, built his butcher shop on the corner of Power and Mellor Streets. In the early 1960s, Tom Ward, one of Matt's butchers bought the property and business. The property is still in the Ward family today.

His small goods prep area was under the single roof, dirt floor, out in the back yard.

Chillor Cauley and Henry Lane did their trade there and were the makers of all the small goods. My parents used to buy their meat from Matt, who was a close friend of my dad.

Matt's youngest daughter, Bernice, was close friends with my youngest sister, Beth. Bernice passed away in December 2021.

Smallgoods work area at rear of butcher shop

I was a mate to Matt's eldest son, Archie; he was a pilot in the 2nd World War. His Liberator had been badly damaged by air flack over Germany, and they were losing height. He asked his crew to bail out over the English Channel, but they refused and said they would stay together. The plane just made the perimeter of the airfield in England, but caught the fence on landing and crashed. Only three survived. Archie was badly injured. I visited him when he came home, he just wasted away with regret and passed in 1946.

In 1984 I called in to the butcher shop now an army disposal store. The walk-in refrigerator doors had been removed and it was full of army gear.

Strange; the shops are still there today, even the two built-in refrigerators are still in place.

Mr Joe Lobb had his Butcher Shop in Tozer Street, opposite the Gympie Railway Railmotor Sheds in 1921.

Joe Lobb - Butcher

In 2020 the front glass window still stated J. Lobb Butcher. It is now covered by the Sauers Nursery sign. Lobb's butcher shop closed in 1939, though this shop also has the meat hangers in situ. Sauers are the owners of the building. The front corner of the awning has been bent like this for at least 60 years. The Judo Club were tenants for 66 years. For the last 14 years, the premises have stood empty.

Mr Gibson of Stewart Terrace had twin boys, David and Laurie, they did their trade under their Father. David married Brickie Thomson's youngest daughter, Marjorie, the baker's oven builder, close friends of my parents.

Gibson's Butcher Shop

The Gibson boys sold out to Nolan Meats in 1968. Henry Lane from Lane's butcher shop was put in as manager after the sale of his shop. In 1996 Pat Nolan sold the shop to Jeff Buckley who had to close the doors at Christmas 2021.

Henry Lane –Butcher - photo 2018

Henry Lane built this building at 18 Duke Street in 1952 and sold to Eric Herbert who had owned Amamoor Butcher. He sold to My Butcher in 1983.

There was a butcher shop at Mount Pleasant, opposite the Post Office.

Another later on in River Road, he lasted two years. It was turned into a Garage. In 2020 it is an Accountancy Firm.

Shaw's Meats, on the corner of Crescent Road and Apollonian Vale, is now a fruit shop.

Shaw's, then Nolan's, Meats - photo 2018

In 1946, a Butcher Shop was opened in Smithfield Street, now known as the Meat Hall.

Gomersall's in Mary Street was sold to Jerry Garrard in 1946. He had been employed by Gomersall's for many years. He changed the name to Garrard's Quality Meats and stayed next door to Harry's Town shop for 4 more years, then moved further down the street, where they had built a new shop opposite Big Bargain Furniture and stayed there until they closed in 1987. These shops were demolished to make way for a new building to be constructed on the site. An electrical Store took over one half of the complex and Cut-Price Groceries the other.

Nolan's Meats took over the Meat Shop operated by Shaw's in the Centro Complex and also at Apollonian Vale.

Goldfields Plaza Shopping Centre in Nash Street had a butcher shop called The Meat Hall.

The South Side have a new Butcher Shop built diagonally opposite Mrs. McDonald's shop.

At the new shopping centre supermarkets, they also put in their own Butcher Shops, all to capture the shopper's trade.

Chapter 24

Cake Icing

Cake icing was an art that I was taught very early in my apprenticeship. At age 16, Harry Brothers sent me off to the Gympie School of Arts in Nash Street, to learn the finer art of cake icing.

Over the next 27 years, I iced many cakes — Wedding, Birthday, Anniversary, Christening, Christmas, and Easter, to name just a few.

Icing is an art of its own. In my mind I can still see Ted and I coming up with lovely designs, colours that were easy on the eyes. I am showing you only a few of the hundreds we designed and sold.

I specialised in bridgework, some cakes taking three to four days to finish. I remember when working in Brisbane, I took an order for two iced wedding cakes. On delivery day, Rosalyn was nursing the main bottom cake as we delivered the cakes, I had to stop at the end of a local street that joins Sandgate Road. I saw an entry space and took off.

Rosalyn caught the cake in her arms; words could not contain my facial expression. A quick trip home, repair, and re-icing on one side. The cake turned out well. The down loops were easy, the up loops took a little longer.

I presented to the archives at the Gympie library, my beautiful book printed in 1937 in London on cake icing, by Joseph Lambeth — the bridgework is remarkable.

I also presented all my work tools such as Metal Nipples, Metal Syringes, bags, and rough designs to the Gympie Historical Society at Monkland, they are now all on show, for young people to see what it was like before plastic.

Wedding Cakes

Our Wedding Cake

Wedding Cakes

Replica cake celebrating 50 years of marriage

Celebration Cakes

Birthday Cake

Bon Voyage

Buttercream Rose Cake

Buttercream Specials

Child's Cake

Merry Christmas

Cake Novelties

Decorated Mints

Easter Cake

Easter Eggs

Freehand in Sugar

Good Luck Cake

Narcissus Cake

Pansy Cake

Poppy Cake

Special Pastries

Stork Cake

Chapter 25

Bakeries that have come and gone in Gympie and District.

In the following years from 1867, ever so many bakeries have started and then in time, slowly disappeared into the woodwork, so they say. As I drive around Gympie and the district, with buildings no longer in existence, I picture the bakeries and bakers standing. Same with the railway cuttings, I can see the old trains puffing around the bends, where the new line now cuts across the valley.

From Brisbane to Cairns, from Mackay to Birdsville, and in the Capital cities across Australia, the story is the same, the big central bakeries bought out the smaller ones and either closed them down or used them as Depots. The bigger supermarkets were putting in place their own hot bread shops.

Customers didn't want to traipse all over town to specialty shops for their everyday needs. They found it much easier to buy all their needs in one shop. The adults in the household are usually both working, no one is home anymore to collect the delivery orders of meat, bread, or green-grocer, as it was when I was young.

William Thomas Weller, closed their last bakery 1909.

John Russell, closed 1909.

Thomas Condie, Mary Street closed down 1934.

Henry Long, sold in 1936.

Neil Bradford, Bakery and Home was burnt down in 1936, not replaced.

Isaac Branch, sold 1936.

First Amamoor Bakery, closed 1936.

Blakeway's Bakery, sold 1944.

Reg Sherran and Sons, sold 1948.

W & J Condie, sold in 1952.

Condie Brothers, closed 1956.

Kandanga Bakery, closed 1957.

Gunalda Bakery, closed 1957.

Kilkivan Bakery, closed 1963.

Imbil Bakery, closed 1964.

Pomona Bakery, closed 1964.

Thomas Condie, Stewart Terrace sold 1965.

Tin Can Bay Bakery 1965

Fred Weller, Monkland closed 1965.

Goomeri Bakery (original), closed 1966.

Woolooga Bakery, 1967.

James Fardoolie closed down 1968.

Kathleen Harry, Reef Street 1968.

Amamoor Bakery Number 2, closed 1969.

Reg Harry/Harry's Brothers, Duke Street closed down 1970.

Bill Dunmore, liquidated 1972.

Many of these towns have replaced their bread supply, with Hot bread shops. My records state the original Bakehouses, as I remember them.

It was hard work, especially when we had internally wood fired ovens and the ovensmen had the responsibility of not burning the bread and only being paid an extra 5/- (50c), on top our £4/- /- ($8) a week wage for the privilege. Then, you worked till all the work was completed for the day.

Chapter 26

Special Memories

In 1937 when Dad and his two mates (Harry and Jack) were recalled back into the PMG they found the Gympie system in a mess. No work had been completed or even started since 1929. The lines were suffering from eight years of neglect.

Lilleys, the GMC Chev dealer in Gympie on the Corner of Mary and Shannon Streets had in their showroom on display a Black, FX Holden. The first Australian made car. A cost of £618 ($1,236). If you could afford one, you ordered your vehicle, paid for it in advance and it was delivered in nine months.

I once told my dad, that I wanted to be an owner someday, and it came into being at Amamoor in 1949, when I was 19 years old.

Our baking trays and tins would have special treatment because of the build-up of dripping. Doug and I would lay them out on the ground and with a mop and boiling water we would coat them all in caustic soda, wash them off with town water (43psi) and allow them to dry. Then stack them all in the bakehouse ready for use the next day.

Today, the bakers have it much easier, because all trays and tins are made from stainless steel and don't need the care that we had to give ours.

Cleaning the Bakery

The choice of cleansing material depends on the nature of the dirt and the surface to be cleaned.

Hot soapy water is the most used cleanser in the bakery. It acts by loosening the flour and such easily soluble things as sugar and by emulsifying the fats; that is, it breaks up fats and greases into very fine particles and keeps them in that state while they are rinsed away. For benches, tools and equipment soap is highly suitable.

Water that will not easily form a lather with soap is said to be "hard". There are two types of hardness: "temporary hardness" and "permanent hardness". The temporary hardness is easily removed by boiling. "Permanent hardness" is due to the presence of lime and magnesium salts which are not affected by boiling. It can be removed by the addition of washing soda, or soda ash which is a triple strength washing soda.

For the inside of the sponge machine or cleaning a bowl for meringues where there must be not even a trace of grease, there are chemical cleaners on the market, technically known as "de-greasers" and "industrial detergents". These are very efficient and give a clean rinse.

Caustic Soda is the most alkaline of all cleaning materials, but it is not a good emulsifier. It is used with hot water where a lot of grease has to be removed and where perfect de-greasing is not necessary. It is a good "wetting" agent. It gets under the grease and down to the surface but it is a little severe on aluminium and tinned surfaces over a period.

Caustic soda should be used only in very weak solutions, even then it is very hard on the hands. It should not be used where it could leave a taste to affect food. Its best use is for floors where a mop or broom can be used.

Ceiling and walls should receive a periodical lime wash, unless, of course, they are painted and have a washable surface.

In some bakeries where a pressure of steam is available, the floors are cleaned with a steam jet — a length of steam hose fitted with about three feet of $\frac{1}{2}$ in. piping. This is efficient on wood, cement or brick floors.

After I had sold Amamoor, I discussed with the Bread Manufacturers of Qld in Brisbane my idea of travelling and relieving bakers for a month while they had a well-earned holiday ... I was swamped with callers.

We bought a bond wood Caramar van. Those days, when you bought a van, all it had inside was a sink, a drop-down dining table for the ¾ size bed, a mattress for the aforesaid bed, a small wardrobe 18" (46cm) wide x 5' (1.52m) high with a bench attached for cosmetics, no stove and 2 bunk beds. That was it! So, we set to and started altering it to suit us.

The bottom bunk was converted to a storage area containing a water tank and an ice chest and room for ports et.,. the top bunk was converted into Lyn's cot.

Parked at Esk bakery for 1 month.

We still had the Singer utility that we did not sell with the bakery, but I bought a 1939 Chevrolet Sedan, a lovely car with coil springs for comfort.

I relieved in bakehouses at Caloundra, Indooroopilly, Stanthorpe, Dulacca, and Esk for 6 months only stopping when Rosalyn's younger brother, Ron, was called up for National Service and Pa needed help with timber logging. We moved in with Granny Rospigaroff at 9 Iron Street.

L-R: Tip Curry, John Stark at Stanthorpe 1953

I have already mentioned what happened to Ted and Joyce Harry up to the time we worked a night together at Nudgee bakery. After that, we lost track of their movements.

In 1972, Rosalyn and I purchased a new unit at Bellara on Bribie Island for the odd weekend away. We had been there about seven months and as we drove around the island sightseeing, we saw this little tea house selling bread and cakes in amongst the shops at the Jetty on the calm side of Bribie and stopped in.

Imagine our surprise when Joyce came to the counter. She hugged us and sang out to Ted to come out and see who she had found. He came out from the little bakehouse attached to the rear of the shop. It was a wonderful reunion.

Joyce had forgiven Ted and they were remarried at Roma, before seeing this little café for sale. Trade had gone through the roof since the new bridge had been built across from the mainland. Their sad news was that they had lost their 14-year old son to a disease that rarely raises its head in Brisbane. Their other son was married and had two boys. He was living and working in Brisbane.

We saw them often, as we called in each time we came up to our unit. On one visit, Joyce told us she had terminal cancer; her cancer had laid dormant for years but now had come back and was incurable. They had no trouble selling the shop, and three months later, we were there when Joyce was buried in the Bribie Island Cemetery.

Ted could not handle his grief and alcohol took over again. He used to sit at the end of the Bribie Bowls Club bar and literary drank his life away.

A few years later, we were travelling from our orchard at Bapaume, Stanthorpe and called into the Bowls Club to hopefully see him. The barman told us that he had passed away a few years before and was buried with Joyce.

I have heard nothing since that day I spent talking to his nieces, Beryl and Janine. They hadn't had any contact with them at all, and all they knew was Ted and Joyce's surviving son still lives somewhere in Brisbane.

Kidd Street Bridge, 1955 Flood

Gympie, as always, is plagued with floods, sometimes they cut all roads in and out of town. Not as bad since the higher bridges were built. Originally the old Normandy Bridge was only 6' (1.8m) above the water.

The water depth almost covering Kidd bridge is at 25' (7.62m), the new bridge was built 5' (1.5m) higher to the left of this one and is called The Channon Street Bridge, after the street that starts there and runs back though the city.

The Gympie Police Station now takes up the corner where Fred Cox's home and Mr Chapple's home and business once stood. Mr Chapple's home was connected by a verandah to his little shop on the corner. The shop was sold to Fred Nash and so it became known as Nash's Corner Store.

Gympie Floods 1955

Gilliland's Garage in Mellor Street where my dad used to buy his petrol at 1/9d (19c) a gallon, was bought by Tom Madill.

The Cassidy boys, Viv and Roy, had taken over their father's mechanical workshop on the corner of Nash and Monkland streets. The Atlantic Hotel drive through bottle-o is now on that corner.

The boys bought the vacant property opposite corner and built a big tin shed for their workshop. I often went to their workshop with my dad during the 1930s, when Dad and Harry Young had their bread vendor delivery vans serviced. After Vic passed away, Roy sold the Garage to a Tyre Company who is still there today in 2022. Roy then had Dave English senior build another workshop and home on the Northern outskirts of Gympie, on the road to Maryborough. Roy Cassidy passed away in 1990. Both the Cassidy boys married, neither of them had any children. I remember Roy's wedding day in August 1942, at Surface Hill Church.

Entrance to Grand Hotel's Air Raid Shelter. Photo 1965.

Roy and Winn Cassidy's Wedding Day. On right is Winn's brother Trevor Edward. Photo 1942.

When I retired back to Gympie and joined the Gympie and District Historical Society, would you believe Roy Cassidy was the Treasurer. I had him do my car services at his workshop till he sold out to the present owners.

The beautiful Grand Hotel on the corner of Mellor and Chapple Streets had to be demolished, because a mine shaft collapsed under the building, and it caved in.

Grand Hotel

The last Air Raid Shelter still in existence in Gympie is located behind the Mines Department Building (now The Gympie Country Music Home) in Channon Street and used as a storeroom for important papers.

We had many of these shelters, the Council built three concrete air raid shelters to the left of the Memorial Park's main gates and the gates were removed to allow access.

The two on the footpath at the Railway Station outside the 'sign on office' for the Railway workshop staff and train crews.

The main Mary Street Air Raid Shelter was in the heart of town. The entrance was in Smithfield Street to "Nash's Gully" beside Carey's Silk Store. I can still see this stairway going down close to the wall. It's a huge brick and cement drainage for all storm water.

Air Raid practice was at 11am every Monday morning. The huge Air Raid siren on the Fire Brigade Building blasted its warning out and everybody had to obey. School teachers and children ran to the nearby slit trenches. Shops closed their doors and headed to their nearest shelter. It continued for 15 minutes, a five-minute break then the all-clear would sound. Only essentials workers were exempt.

The Memorial Park was completely enclosed by a high fence and the rear fences of the Zoo's cages were 6' (1.8m) away from the River Road fence. The zoo had monkeys, birds, and much more, but the monkeys are fore front in my memory of the zoo. We used to be able to buy a bag of peanuts and feed them to the monkeys.

Each afternoon, the caretaker of the Memorial Park would ring a hand bell for 5 minutes so everybody had time to vacate the park before he closed the main Gates in Reef Street at 5.45 pm. Ladies took over the care of the park when the men went to war.

The zoo also closed at the start of the 2nd World War. I don't know what happened to the animals, but the cages were slowly demolished.

The fence was also later removed, and the park has never been enclosed since.

Rowe's General store and Newsagency was located three doors up from the corner of Power and Mellor Street. I went to school with his daughter Shirley. Mr Rowe delivered our Sunday Mail, Gympie Times, and Courier Mail by push bike for 20 years.

In the gold rush days, Gympie had 46 Hotels (nearly one on every corner). Hotels had plenty of customers. In those years, closing time was at 6pm. Today we have only 12 in Gympie, and they now close at 10pm, unless under the new laws they have a nightclub attached and can stay open until 3am.

Many hotels were burnt down, some that I remember were The Mining Exchange, The Northumberland, The Columbia, and The Jubilee.

The boarding Houses of Gympie that I can vividly remember were Mrs Murphy's home in Crescent Road. The Railway Refreshment Rooms Single Ladies Quarters in Lady Mary Terrace. The Mellor Street boarding house opposite Edgar Rowe's Newsagency and there were many more that have faded from my memory.

1940s Boarding House in Mellor Street opposite Rowes Newsagency. Photo 2018.

Fred Murray's home in Channon Street. Photo 1931.

The beautiful Queenslander homes of Cullinane's in Channon Street and Murray's in Channon Street are no longer there.

The Catholic buildings on Calton Hill, and many private residences on Red Hill, Horse Shoe Bend, and Lady Mary Terrace. Many of which are still standing.

All these changes were going on over many years and we were growing older as the town grew bigger.

In 1983, Clyde Kunst, Irv Runge, Bill Smith-Godwin, Tom Smith, and myself, all started at the Gympie and District Historical Society to give Gympie two years voluntary service. We left 13 years later in 1996.

L-R: John Stark, Tom Smith, Clyde Kunst, Irv Runge, Bill Smith-Godwin. Photo 1985.

Our greatest challenges were the rebuilding of the huge wooden Poppet Head and Gantry. The complete restoration of the big 1897 Walkers Steam Engine and the steam driven Compressor, Electric Generator and Battery Building.

My greatest reward was the recommissioning of the Steam Locomotive No45 which we removed from Tozer Park. I personally reduced this locomotive to pieces. My friends, the Commissioners of Queensland Railways, Ralph Sheahy and Vince O'Rourke, were very generous to our society, repairing and making parts no longer available.

Rosalyn and I visited all the locomotives in Parks and Sugar Mills, from Dover in Tasmania to Alice Springs and anyone and everyone else who had Queensland Rolling Stock, to try and procure the missing parts we needed. No45 has 46 identical parts in her restoration. I collected rolling stock so I could show school children what it was like when I was a boy.

Photo of #45 one week before re-commissioning to main line operation. Photo 1992

The Engine was recommissioned on the 12th of October 1992, on Gympie's 125th Birthday.

We fired this locomotive four times a week. Jack Ison joined me in driving No 45. Jack told stories of his years of being an engine driver for Queensland Rail. He loved this task as much as I.

To be able to achieve the restoration of the locomotive, I had to study and become a steam engineer to be proficient to make and service steam gear. Many long nights of study. I finally succeeded and had all the necessary Certificates and qualifications to be able to do any steam restoration.

All of my 13 years of work at the Mining Museum was voluntary. Rosalyn and I also donated the cost of our travelling expenses looking for parts. When parts were needed on No 45 I donated a lot of steam fittings from my personal collection.

In 1995, after twice having all our equipment in the Museum Railway Stages 1 and 2 under water from the flooding of the Mary River. That caused a lot of extra work for my crew. Thank goodness Railway Rolling stock are all screwed and bolted together.

I was in touch with the then Railway Commissioner Mr. Vince O'Rourke, trying to obtain the Monkland Railway Station and yards, so we could transfer all the railway stock and equipment above flood water when I was approached by Jim Walker from the local Apex Club in Gympie with an idea to run a tourist train up the Mary Valley Line to Brooloo. I thought that was a great idea.

But we had no connection for the Locomotive and all the Carriages from the Museum to the main line at Monkland. What's more, the Museum would be losing a great attraction.

Some weeks later we had another flood, and the water was 3" (7.62cm) over the foot plate of the Locomotive and the Carriage Roofs were all that stood out of the flood. That did it! I called Jim and discussed the problem, and the rest is history. The Mary Valley Heritage Rail became a reality. You can read all about it in my book *The Return of Steam Locomotive No 45.*

Jack and I then turned our skills to building the new brick double storey theatre and administration block below the water tank. The Gympie and District Historical Societies main viewing building of displays. We completed the new building in 7 months.

In 1959, I joined my brother-in-law and became a Master Builder. Following this, I went out and worked on my own. In 1968 I purchased a Plastic Factory in Stafford, Brisbane. This was a Sydney based company, selling their Queensland plant, and returning to the Sydney. I was a person in the right place at the right time being in both steam and plastic. While doing all this, life was going on.

From 1936 to 2014, I collected Gympie Times clippings that were of interest to me. I had 11½ bushel cases of clippings, which, when I finally donated it to the Gympie Library, were 29 double sided 500mm x 300mm heavy laminated pages in books of ten pages. The library in turn scanned them all into their computer archives for safe keeping.

The Railway Complex at the Museum was produced for Gympie's 125th year's celebrations. The Gympie Times cuttings were finished for Gympie's 150th celebrations.

I must admit I waffle on a little. But I have so much to say and write about. I wish to repeat a poem I have known since a boy. This conveys my message perfectly. I have placed the poem at the end of the book.

I had a copy enlarged and framed and presented it to Winston House, a Presbyterian Aged Care Centre in Channan Street. It was hung in the main hallway to the dining room.

Now closed many years, the Centre was converted into units and sold by the Uniting Church. I was not given the opportunity to reclaim the framed poem, when everything was disposed of. The Uniting Church also sold the huge Surface Hill Church complex.

The Museums of Gympie encompassed my life, especially the Historical and Mining and the Forestry Museum. So much history available to see and a drive around Gympie will show a lot more to you. I am sure you will enjoy your trip.

I have given you in previous books the story of our beautiful High School.

I could go on talking for hours of the places and people I have known, worked and sang with. Scouts, Cubs, The Air Training Corp, and Choirs.

Being the only Marriage Celebrant in Gympie for ten years, I still run into couples I married and sometimes get introduced to their children as well. I have been a Justice of the peace since 1974.

I hold and treasure five Life Memberships from Gympie organizations.

I have been a local Preacher since I was 16 in the Methodist, Uniting, and The Union Churches and all churches who have invited me into their pulpits to preach the Gospel of Jesus Christ. I only gave it away in the last eight years, owing to my age.

Over time, all this has now passed, as it should. We now go forward with these memories to give us and our children the strength to learn from what we dealt with in the past and to do better with the future. I have loved being your servant and fellow traveller along life's way.

My Ros and I at the beach. Photo 1950

Where Channon Street meets Mary Street. Photo 1931

Looking down to the Fiveways from Calladonian Hill. Photo 1931

Mary Street from Channon Street. Photo 1931

View from Horseshoe Bend. Photo 1931

Where the Gympie Brisbane Road starts. Photo 1931

Nostalgia

Remember the cheese of my childhood and
the bread we cut with a knife,
When children helped with the housework;
the man went to work,
not the wife.
The cheese never needed an ice-chest, and
the bread was so crusty and hot.
The children were seldom unhappy; the wife
was content with her lot.

I remember the milk from the billy, with the
yummy cream on the top.
Our dinner came from the oven and not from
the fridge at the shop.
I remember the shop on the corner, where a
penny's worth of lollies were sold.
Do you think I'm a bit too nostalgic, or is it
I'm just growing old?

The kids were much more contented; they
didn't need money for "kicks".
Just a game with their mates in the paddock,
and sometimes
the Saturday flicks.
Our simple home-made toys came from
items previously used.
Whittling a stick was much fun; took little to
keep us amused.

I remember when the loo was a dunny and
the pan man came in the night,
It wasn't the least bit funny, going out the
back with no light.

The clothes were boiled in a copper with
plenty of rich foaming suds.
But the ironing seemed never-ending as
Mum pressed everyone's duds.

I remember the slap on the backside and the
taste of soap if I swore.
Anorexia and diets weren't heard of, we
hadn't much choice what we wore.
Do you think that bruised our egos, or our
initiative quite destroyed?
We ate what was put on the table, and life
was better enjoyed.

Poet Unknown

Our Family: - John, Jenelle, Ken, Lynette, Trevor, Rosalyn. Photo 1993

John Stark

List of Previously Published Books:

Memories of Gympie during the War Years 1939 – 1945

John Stark My years at the Central State Schools 1934 – 1942

The Return of Steam Locomotive C17, No. 45

List of Works

"It Seems Like a Dream" My Years at the Gympie State High school – 1942 – 1945

My Scrapbooks

www.ingramcontent.com/pod-product-compliance
Lightning Source LLC
Chambersburg PA
CBHW071908290426
44110CB00013B/1318